HarperCollins*Publishers*
1 London Bridge Street
London SE1 9GF
www.harpercollins.co.uk

First published by HarperCollins*Publishers* 2017

13 5 7 9 10 8 6 4 2

Text © Christopher Sjuve, 2017
Photography © Erik Hannemann, 2017

Thanks to Elisabet Skårberg, Jon Tore Modell, Maria Stangeland, Karl Fredrik Tangen, Ingunn Haraldsen, Morten Ståle Nilsen and Einar Røhnebæk. Thanks to Anita Holthe. And thanks to everyone who tries the recipes!

Christopher Sjuve asserts the moral right to be identified as the author of this work
A catalogue record of this book is available from the British Library

ISBN 978-0-00-826352-2
Printed and bound at GPS Group

Cook's Notes: **Bacon:** The bacon used in the recipes is smoked bacon, unless otherwise specified. **Eggs:** Eggs are medium sized throughout. **Oven temperatures:** For fan ovens, reduce the temperature by 20°C. However, refer also to the manufacturer's handbook for your particular oven. **Measurements:** Both metric and imperial measurements are given. Follow either set of measures, not a mixture, as they are not interchangeable.

THE
BACON
BOOK

CHRISTOPHER SJUVE

THE
BACON
BOOK

Irresistible, mouthwatering recipes!

PHOTOGRAPHY: ERIK HANNEMANN

HarperCollins*Publishers*

CONTENTS

Born to love bacon

I'LL NEVER FORGET THE SIGHT. My son – totally uninterested in food up until this point – playing on the floor at his grandparents' house. Suddenly, the bacon hit the frying pan. It was intended for the top of a cauliflower gratin. But then, after a few minutes, came that familiar, wonderful smell that comes whenever heat and bacon are brought together. A smell people have loved since we were still living in caves. Call it a Maillard reaction, call it a miracle … or just call it an irresistible smell. It makes no difference to the magic.

Without warning, in the otherwise silent living room, the boy began to turn around. It was as though some sort of dense magnetic field was dragging him, bodily, out of a world of childish fantasy.

And so, in fully formed words (his vocabulary, unlike his diet, was unusually advanced for his age), he half-stuttered, half-demanded …

'What … what's that beautiful smell?'

And with that, the boy was uncontrollably, irreversibly lost. We're all born with a desire for bacon. All of us. Not raised. Born.

We love bacon. That magical smell of frying bacon is equally irresistible to us all. It's not something taught, or learned – we're born this way.

The appeal of the smell of cooking meat is deeply engrained, and no other cooked meat compares with bacon. Bacon is in a class of its own.

Writing a book about meat right now is at odds with the Zeitgeist. No smart person on earth would seriously deny that we should be eating less meat, and quite rightly so. Meat production consumes huge amounts of space and energy, and we know full well that it's bad for the planet.

At the same time, most people aren't going to stop eating meat altogether. Which is where bacon comes in: bacon gives more bang for the buck than any other sort of meat. A few rashers of bacon in a pasta dish with asparagus give it a body and flavour that would be missing without it. Bacon fills a gap, making the dish deliciously filling. It doesn't take much bacon to give a modern, green plate of food that little bit extra. Just a few good, crispy rashers. That's the beauty of bacon.

Some might ask what bacon can be used for, but the answer to that question could go on forever. Instead, we can turn the question back on itself: what *isn't* bacon good for? Sushi? Dessert? Drinks? Nope. Not if you use it properly.

It's difficult to argue with bacon's sheer, fabulous versatility. The point of this book is very simple: everything does taste better with bacon.

Christopher

CHRISTOPHER SJUVE

«*That magical smell of frying bacon is equally irresistible to us all. It's not something taught, or learned, we're born this way.*»

Before

After

In search of the first rasher of
BACON
TEN PIGS BY THE TIGRIS

A MAN CROUCHES behind a rock and raises his arm silently. He has a spear clutched firmly in his right hand, tipped with the sharpest stone he could find. In the clearing before him a pig is grunting with pleasure, burrowing eagerly into some promising roots. It's lost in the task, paying no heed to its surroundings.

The hunter rises to his feet to get enough power behind the throw, lifting himself into a standing position as slowly, as carefully, as he can. The moment has come.

It happens fast. He tenses his body, hurling the spear with all the strength he can muster. The pig senses something is wrong the moment the spear leaves the hunter's hand. It suddenly stops digging and turns its head to face the hunter, their eyes meeting for a fraction of a second. Moving by reflex alone, the pig leaps forward, escaping the deadly projectile by millimetres. It squeals loudly and within seconds it disappears into the bushes, out of sight. The hunter listens as it escapes into the forest. The proud hunter slouches home, tired, hungry and frustrated. He knows that his children are even hungrier than he is. 'Story of my life,' he mutters to himself. 'It's bad for me and it's worse for the kids.' It's been days since he brought home any meat.

The next morning, he wakes feeling strangely determined. He's had enough. He's sick of chasing his prey through the woods. The pigs are fast and persistent and nigh-impossible to outwit. They can literally smell him coming, long before he can so much as lay eyes on them. There must be a smarter way to do this. There must be some way to avoid this constant need to hunt, while still getting to have as much meat as he wants.

This weary, frustrated man lived by the river Tigris, and it's him we have to thank for bacon. It may have taken another 1,000 years or more before we were tucking into rashers of thin bacon for breakfast, but without pigs, there would be no bacon.

«You can salt and smoke rashers of beef, mutton, goat, reindeer, moose or rabbit, as much as you like, but they'll never be bacon.»

Tigris

IRAN

Man

Bacon is made from pork. End of story. You can't make bacon from anything else. You can salt and smoke rashers of beef, mutton, goat, reindeer, moose or rabbit as much as you like, but they'll never be bacon. That frustrated hunter from the Tigris was the first to successfully domesticate pigs and that's why we owe him so much. He was the first to truly make pigs his own.

DOMESTICATION

Taming a pig is a bit like taming a cat. Harder than taming a sheep, but a little easier than taming a horse, which needs to be ridden before it can be brought under control. That, at least, is unnecessary with a pig. The animal's trust needs to be won slowly but steadily, with food, treats and warm scratches behind the ears. Eventually, a friendship between man and pig develops. It's a special bond, characterised by affection, kindness and regular meals. But, eventually, the free board and lodgings hold a price for the pig.

We don't know exactly when pigs started to become household animals – it seems to have developed at different times in both Europe and Asia. But we know that it was a very long time ago. Archaeological discoveries in modern Germany suggest that humans have been keeping pigs for more than 11,000 years and it seems to have developed independently in numerous other societies, all over the world.

Pigs weren't the first animals to be domesticated – unlike sheep, they can't subsist on grass and leaves alone. They require a more varied diet. It was only after we figured out how to feed pigs that we could domesticate them and estimates of when this happened vary wildly. Some sources suggest that it was as long as 13,000

years ago. We've found evidence of pigs dating back 11,400 years on Cyprus, and it's safe to say that they didn't get there by themselves. In China, we know that pig-keeping was commonplace at least 8,000 years ago. Pigs have also lived in close proximity to humans for many years. The history of man's relationship with pigs is the beginning of the story of bacon.

SALTING MEAT

The story of bacon begins, naturally enough, with pigs. But it takes more than pork to make bacon. We need salt, and we need smoke. The oldest sources we have concerning salt production are from China. It's not certain if the Chinese were the first to extract salt, but they certainly appear to have been the first to write about it. Unsurprising, perhaps, given that Chinese is the oldest written culture still alive today. The first record of salt production we have is a document from approximately 800 BC describing the salt production and trade taking place at least 1,000 years earlier, during the Xia dynasty. Salt was produced by boiling salt water in earthenware pots until salt crystals formed on the base. Yi Dun is, so far as we can tell, the first person to have begun boiling salt water to produce salt in iron pots, in approximately 450 BC – a far more effective technique than using earthenware pots.

It's unlikely that the Chinese discovered how to salt meat. Salt was expensive and sprinkling large amounts of it on pork must have seemed like a colossal waste of time and resources. Salt was used to make fish sauce, by fermenting small fish in salt. This sauce, known as 'jiang', was used as seasoning. Eventually, someone discovered that you can mix soya beans with the fish, and eventually the fish was dropped completely, giving us 'jiangyou': soy sauce.

Of course, we can't rule out the possibility that some other Chinese people, some other time, took something like pork belly and salted, sliced, fried and ate it. But, if so, it never became a hit.

«We've found evidence of pigs dating back 11,400 years on Cyprus, and it's safe to say that they didn't get there by themselves.»

« Remember, the next time you look at the pyramids, that they couldn't have been built without the help of bacon. Makes you think, doesn't it? »

DID THE EGYPTIANS MAKE BACON?

The Egyptians could have been the first. They'd certainly mastered the art of domesticating pigs – and ducks, pelicans, geese and quail, for that matter – and they made valiant, if unsuccessful, efforts to tame antelopes and various types of gazelle. You certainly can't say they didn't try. But it wasn't just domestication – they had salt, too. Lots of salt. They used a different method from the Chinese boiling – as a desert people, they knew how to use the sun's energy to evaporate the salt water of the Nile Delta.

There were a lot of domesticated pigs in ancient Egypt, and they left plenty of archaeological evidence behind. The oldest finds date back to 5,000 BC, and pig farming would appear to have continued more or less continuously throughout the classical era. The bulk of these archaeological discoveries has been found in the graves of the lower classes, indicating that pork may have been primarily a poor man's food – possibly for builders, even slaves.

The first pyramids were constructed using vast numbers of people, whose diet, archaeological evidence suggests, was primarily meat-based. Archaeologists have dug up the bones of cows, sheep, goats … and pigs. Fewer pigs than the other animals, admittedly – it may be that some of the lower classes ate salted pork. Which brings us closer to bacon – so remember, the next time you look at the pyramids, that they couldn't have been built without the help of bacon. Makes you think, doesn't it?

We know for certain that the Egyptians understood the art of preserving meat and fish with salt, so it wasn't a lack of knowledge that held them back from discovering bacon. There was, however, an aversion to pork among the upper classes. It is believed that the reasons for this may have been religious, as well as cultural, but either way there's still no reason why the Egyptians couldn't have been the first. But they weren't. Even back in the time of the pharaohs, it seems that pigs weren't regarded well in the Middle East.

The Chinese eventually discovered other ways of producing salt, including mining, but it was the boiling method that eventually spread westwards. The Romans adopted this technique around 1,000 years after the Chinese first wrote about it, and it spread throughout the Roman Empire. Long before the rise of Rome, the Romans had mastered everything to do with salt. Then, they went on to conquer the salt people.

THE CELTS – MYSTICAL SALT PEOPLE

Existing in parallel with the Roman Empire were the barbarians (the Romans referred to everyone who lived outside of their Empire as barbarians, albeit not necessarily with the same negative connotations that the word carries today), and among the most important of the barbarian peoples were the Celts. There remains an aura of mystery and uncertainty around the Celts, primarily because they left behind no written sources. What we do know, however, from numerous archaeological discoveries, is that theirs was a rich culture, skilled in trade, livestock and, not least, salt.

The Greeks called the people living to the north of the Roman Empire 'keltoi'. The Romans called them 'galli', or Gauls, while the Egyptian version was 'hal' – which means salt. The Celts were the salt people.

Strabo (63 BC–24 AD)

Whenever you find a town called Hall-something-or-other, it's more than likely that you're looking at a Celtic settlement – a town where salt was extracted. The most famous of these is Hallstatt, where a huge prehistoric salt mine, filled with archaeological riches, has been found.

According to Mark Kurlansky's book *Salt*, the Celts quickly learned that there was much to be gained from selling not just salt but salted meat, too. Salted meat was a Celtic speciality, known throughout Europe and the outer edges of the ancient world.

We know of the Celts' love of pork from two ancient, unconnected historians from Greece. Strabo (63 BC –24 AD) observed that the Celts were fond of ham, especially from domesticated animals. They may well have developed the forerunner to Parma ham, for example, and they didn't stop there. The second historian, Athenaios, writing 200 years later, tells that the Celts seemed to have a particular love of the upper cuts of ham, which brings us perilously close to that all-important pork belly. It's interesting that Athenaios felt that this distinction was worth pointing out. The difference between a cut of meat from the upper or lower part of the leg isn't especially great in itself, but as soon as you reach the belly, the meat becomes much fattier. This makes the distinction more worthy of note. It's as though the historian is trying to tell us that the Celts almost loved bacon but missed by a few centimetres – perhaps due to a lack of precise terminology, culinary understanding, or anatomical knowledge.

In summary: the Celts loved pork, were specialists in both salt and the art of salting meat, and they loved the upper part of the leg. It's more than likely that the Celts made bacon – or, at least, something very like unsmoked bacon. It's also not improbable that the Romans learned to make bacon, perhaps by figuring it out for themselves, perhaps by learning it from the Celts.

The Romans made something called petaso, often cited as a sort of forerunner to bacon. Petaso was, at least according to Apicius' cookbook, made from the foreleg, or shoulder. It was boiled with figs for several hours, before being grilled and served with pepper. It's not easy to see what this has to do with bacon, although I don't doubt that it was tasty.

Another Roman source gives us a clearer idea of what the Romans actually ate. In Cato the Elder's book on agriculture, which includes a good deal of practical information about wine-making, olive pressing,

«*Given that the Romans were also known for salting and for raising pigs, they certainly had access to all three of the magic ingredients for making bacon.*»

animal husbandry and the like, the entire final chapter is devoted to salting ham. There are detailed descriptions of how the meat should be completely covered with salt, that it should be turned after a few days and other such practical tips. Then he tells us that the meat should be hung 'over smoke' for two days. He doesn't go into much more detail than that, which suggests that this was a familiar technique that required no elaboration. You get the impression that this was simply something that 'everybody knew'.

In this instance, the instructions are explicitly about ham. But, given that the Romans were also known for salting and for raising pigs, they certainly had access to all three of the magic ingredients for making bacon. Apicius' cookbook includes several – more than several, in fact – references to pork that has been salted (*salsum crudum*), dried and even smoked. There are no actual recipes for anything that might be bacon, and the various types of cured pork are only ever referenced as pre-made ingredients, so details are unfortunately sparse.

The Romans, just like modern Italians, had a knack for coming up with delicious delicacies, so it should be no surprise that at least some of the Roman Empire's numerous farmers, chefs and gourmets would try to salt, smoke and cure pork. It makes sense. They had everything they needed.

Etymology

BACON IS LIFE

THE DEVELOPMENT OF the word 'bacon' seems to have been something of a shared project for Europe. The word exists in English, French, German, Dutch and Norwegian. The road has been bumpy, but today we all agree that the word is bacon.

If you entered an inn 1,000 years ago and ordered bacon and eggs, you certainly wouldn't have been served bacon and eggs. Eggs wouldn't have been a problem, but less certain is what they would have accompanied. Perhaps a steak?

There seems to be general agreement among people who've tried to write the history of bacon that the word can be traced to Old German, where we find the word 'bak'. This evolved into the High German 'bakko' (which can be spelled in numerous ways, including 'bacho'), which can mean either belly or bacon.

The word also appeared in the Netherlands as 'baken' and we know that the French were talking about bacon before the 1600s. In the German vernacular, this would eventually develop into 'bakkon', the equivalent of the English 'back' and the Norwegian 'bak'. So far, so straightforward. Bacon must be about the back. Of a pig. Right?

The only problem here is that bacon is not, in fact, always made using meat from the back. 'Bak' on a pig can mean one of two things – either the back,

or the gammon. This presents us with a problem, because bacon can actually come from the belly – that is the front and the bottom.

In England, back bacon generally refers to the thin rashers of meat carved from the loin at the back of the pig, which makes everything fairly straightforward. But in the USA and Scandinavia bacon comes from the side or belly of the animal, making 'streaky bacon'. This doesn't have much to do with the back. So, what's going on?

When the word bacon entered the English language in the 1100s (from French) it was used in more or less the same way as 'flitch', referring to the salted sides of pork. A few centuries later, the word bacon was generally used for salted pork. There was even a somewhat confusing period when bacon was also used to describe pork in general. This practice lasted until well into the 1800s.

As the years have passed, everyone has thankfully come to general agreement about the meaning of 'bacon'. That is to say, everyone in England. And everyone in the USA. Unfortunately, there's still plenty of confusion between the two.

It was only with the development of modern industry and the need for standardisation that two different types of bacon developed. There is, however, no doubt that the whole thing started in England.

Etymology

ETYMOLOGY IS THE STUDY of the origins of words. The vocabularies of modern languages come from a variety of different sources: some have evolved from older words, others have been borrowed from foreign languages and some have been named from people, developed from initialisms, or even have been deliberately invented by a certain author.

SOURCE: WIKTIONARY.ORG

«In 1805, 6,000 pigs were exported from Ireland. By 1813 this had increased to 14,000 and by 1821 it had reached 104,000.»

Modern
BACON

FOR A LONG time, people made bacon on farms, entirely separately from each other. Everyone would salt and smoke their own meat, just as they would brew their own beer, bake their own bread and make their own jam. It wasn't until the Industrial Revolution hit England that we started to see the sort of modern, mass-produced bacon we find in shops today.

In 17th-century England, pork was a lot less common than it would be a few hundred years later. It wasn't until the arrival of the potato that pig farming really took off, when farmers began to use potatoes as feed. The numbers varied from region to region, but, in the Midlands, as many as 50–60 per cent of farmers were raising pigs and sides of meat could be seen hanging in many a cottage chimney.

Bacon was largely a poor man's food and it was common to keep a few sides of it in the house for emergencies. The ability to store bacon for long periods did more to keep people from stealing than any number of religious ceremonies, threats, penalties and prisons. Bacon helped to hold society together when times were tough. Only the very poorest had to live without the safety net of salted and smoked bacon (that said, it's worth remembering that the word 'bacon' was defined much more broadly in pre-Industrial Revolution England than it is today and could refer to any type of salted pork).

But the times they were a-changing, and by the dawn of the 19th century industrialisation was hammering on the doors of society. In England, at least, one firm in particular was associated with the wide-scale mass production of bacon, founded by brothers John and Henry Harris from the town of Calne.

Picture the scene …

'Hi, Henry!' calls John to his little brother, who is busy weighing salt. It's here, in the back room, that he makes his bacon.

'I've run out of meat for bacon, John. Should we head out and see if we can get some more?'

The brothers pack up their things and get ready to go out. Their bacon is becoming more and more popular, and it wouldn't do for their customers' demand to outstrip supply.

Henry was married to Sophia Perkins and inherited the grocery and butcher's shop from her parents. A few years earlier, John and Henry's father had died, leaving their mother to keep the family shop up and running for a few years before Henry took that over as well.

Meanwhile, John had opened his own shop a little way down the high street. Both of them salted and smoked their own bacon and sold it over the counter.

Luckily, they didn't have to go far to find their ingredients. Calne was a popular stopover for people taking their pigs to London. Many of these pigs had been transported en masse from Ireland – on any given day, as many as 1,400 pigs could pass through Customs in Bristol alone. Along the way, they met up with English pigs that were being transported.

« The ice came from local water whenever it was cold enough in the English villages. When there was no local ice, they imported it from Norway. »

In 1805, 6,000 pigs were exported from Ireland. By 1813 this had increased to 14,000, and by 1821 it had reached 104,000. The figure continued to climb as the advent of steamships made the process ever more efficient. By 1837 as many as 600,000 Irish pigs were turned into food in England.

Pigs held a special position in Ireland. Englishmen travelling to the Emerald Isle reacted with disbelief to the sight of pigs living indoors, right alongside people. And there was no shortage of pigs. Great herds of them – it's estimated that at one point there were as many as 1.4 million. That was before the Potato Famine.

The Irish could get a much better price for their pigs in England. When Englishmen asked how they could let their pigs live together with them, the usual answer was, 'Well, they pay their rent.'

Being a butcher in the little town of Calne wasn't a bad way to make a living. The fattest pigs never stood a chance of making it all the way to London and many died along the way. According to a contemporary witness named George Bowles, '(t)hey just can't cope with the stress of the journey' and it was common to lose as many as 40–50 animals from a large herd.

John and Henry had no difficulty finding pigs to buy. A quick handshake sealed the deal and the fattest pigs, the ones that probably wouldn't have survived the rest of the journey anyway, were easy to barter for. The trade continued to grow steadily, but everything changed for the brothers and their family in the second half of the 1840s. That was when the parasite *Phytophthora infestans* hit the potato crops of Ireland, devastating them. The famine that follwed left millions of people starving to death, and it was similarly catastrophic for pigs, who were largely raised on potatoes.

Once the flow of pigs stopped, the Harris family were presented with something of a problem. They decided to send John's youngest son to America and so George Harris set off on his own adventure. For a full year, he travelled around in search of bacon, which he sent home to Calne. The adventure was at least partly successful and after a quick visit home in 1848 he again set sail across the ocean, determined to establish a bacon factory in Schenectady, New York. He lasted a year before he was forced to throw in the towel and return to the old country.

On the surface, this doesn't sound like a success story. But George's experiences in the USA would prove vital to the future of the Harris family business.

In the USA, George had been introduced to modern cooling techniques. In Calne the sides of bacon would typically be covered in salt for the whole summer. It was easier in winter, when the colder temperatures made it easier to make bacon without risking ruining the meat, but the huge amount of salt required for the summer bacon had clear disadvantages. In the USA, George had seen how vast quantities of ice

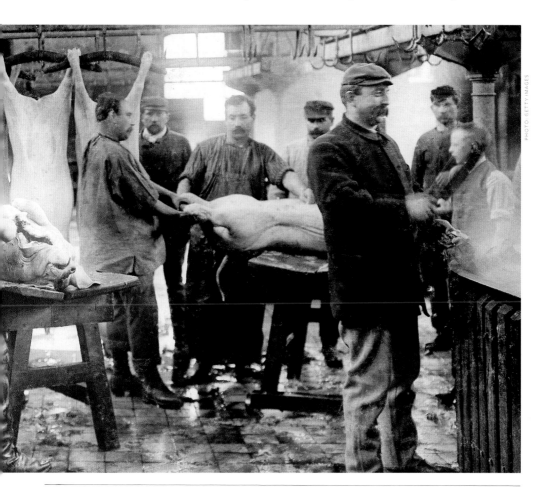

PHOTO: GETTY IMAGES

were used during production and had the brainwave of adopting the same technique at home. The first icehouse was set up in 1856, with the ice being stored in large chambers on an iron floor above the room where the sides of bacon were kept. They found that the cold isolated the room effectively, so started to use it in the walls as well. Later, in 1864, Thomas Harris would actually patent this design of the icehouse.

The ice came from local water, whenever it was cold enough in the English villages. When there was no local ice, they imported it from Norway, where ice was rarely in short supply. All this ice allowed the Harrises to precisely adjust the salt content of their bacon, and before long they were making the best bacon around. They had a huge head start on everyone else, who rapidly started to adopt the same approach. The old form of heavily salted bacon was soon history, making way for what would eventually become known as Wiltshire bacon, a term still in use today. The Harris family were granted an extra honour when they were appointed as official suppliers of bacon to the British royal family.

By now, the Industrial Revolution was in full swing. Pigs were transported from all over England and the flow of pigs from Ireland slowly resumed as the famine-stricken country began to recover. Denmark also began to establish itself as a supplier, and when Germany started to impose tariffs, eventually banning the import of live pigs entirely, the Danes found themselves with 300,000 pigs and nobody to buy them. The animals ultimately ended up in England and thus began a long-lasting trade agreement that further bolstered the production of bacon in Wiltshire and elsewhere in England.

«The Harris family will nonetheless always hold a special place in the history of modern bacon.»

Other producers could build their own icehouses by licensing the design from the Harrises, creating a major new source of income for the family, which they used to further expand and mechanise their facilities. The rate of growth was astonishing – John and Henry's mother would have considered it a good week if she could slaughter as many as five or six pigs and still manage to sell all the carcasses by Saturday, but by 1879 her sons' facilities were processing more than 1,000 pigs a week.

The brothers operated two separate companies for much of the 19th century, but the bonds of family remained tight and in 1888 they consolidated into one large company. They exported bacon to most of Europe, the USA, Australia, India, China and New Zealand, even supplying the steamships that were by now regularly crisscrossing the Atlantic and Pacific oceans.

The company eventually outgrew its humble origins, through buy-outs and steady expansion, and by 1920 ownership was entirely out of the hands of the original Harris family. The Harris family will nonetheless always hold a special place in the history of modern bacon. The extent of their legacy is debatable, as for most major, ground-breaking companies, but it can be convincingly argued that their efforts played a key role in establishing bacon as an iconic product for the modern age.

BACON AND EGG MUFFINS

SEE RECIPE, PAGE 63 »

The first pigs in

AMERICA

'OK, CHRISTOPHER, YOU need to take these pigs with you.'

'But … '

'You aren't listening. I'm the one paying for the voyage. And I assure you, you won't regret it.'

Picture the scene. Christopher Columbus is preparing for his second expedition to the New World, and Queen Isabel of Spain is determined to have her way. She was, after all, a practical woman. From her perspective, his previous voyage had not been a success – after all, he had never made it to India. But the new territories could still be colonised, which soon became policy.

This was why a full flotilla of 17 ships ended up packed with 1,000 people, horses and cows. Alongside them were the first eight pigs to set trotter in the New World. Apparently, it was the Queen herself who insisted that Columbus take pigs with him across the Atlantic.

The pigs reached solid ground in November 1493. The idea was that they would multiply, making future expeditions easier by ensuring a steady supply of meat in the New World. The Spaniards had big plans for the future. We know that Columbus picked the eight pigs up on La Gomera, in the Canary Islands, before setting off and that the cargo included both wild and domesticated pigs. They had no problems surviving the voyage, which was far and away the longest any pig had ever undertaken. There were no pigs in America before Columbus – these were the first. There were other hooved animals, called peccaries, javelina, or skunk pigs, that closely resembled pigs, but with a few differences.

Columbus

America

«It's worth pointing out the striking coincidence that Cortés, de León and de Soto all hailed from the Extremadura region of western Spain and all three had grown up around pigs.»

The imported pigs eventually established a wild population in the West Indies, roaming through the jungles eating everything they came across. They turned out to be well suited to the new environment and thrived on this new, strange fauna. Columbus's pigs would leave their mark on the history of pigs in America. They proved highly adaptable and soon enough there were so many that it started to become a problem. In the years to come the Spanish conquistadors would have their hands full keeping the porcine population in check. It was bad enough that they grazed on the colonists' corn and sugarcane crops, but from time to time they would attack cows and even people when they felt threatened.

Christopher Columbus

More than 40 years later, in 1539, Hernando de Soto launched the first European expedition into the American mainland. His cargo included 2,500 'shoulders of bacon', as well as an unspecified number of live pigs. Some sources mention as many as 200 pigs, while others claim there were as few as 13 sows and two boars. It's similarly uncertain where he obtained the pigs, but some sources maintain that he bought them in Cuba from another conquistador, Ponce de León.

Where had de León got them from, then? It seems likely that they were descendants of the small herd Columbus had brought with him, which may have bred with other pigs that undertook the same voyage later on, but historians aren't certain. Another hypothesis is that de León had brought his own pigs on an expedition to Florida 18 years earlier, but there's no concrete evidence to support this.

De Soto could also have obtained his pigs from Vasco Porcallo de Figueroa. If so, it was probably in exchange for a place for de Figueroa on the expedition team. De Soto's landing in Tampa Bay in Florida was the first time a pig had seen the American mainland. His expedition lasted for many years, crisscrossing much of what is now the South-eastern United States. During this time, the pig population increased to 700 animals, not including those that had escaped captivity or been stolen by Native Americans. There's good reason to believe that these pigs were the ancestors of the wild boars, or razorbacks, that roam the southern States to this day.

Cortés also took pigs with him when he conquered Mexico. It's worth pointing out the striking coincidence that Cortés, de León and de Soto all hailed from the Extremadura region of western Spain and all three had grown up around pigs. In other words, they knew their pigs. This knowledge would prove far more important in America than anyone could have anticipated.

In the years that followed, the Spaniards continued to bring pigs with them across the Atlantic. Some were kept as domestic animals, but many others lived wild. They provided meat for the conquistadors, but also brought with them infections to which the Europeans were immune, but that proved fatal to

the native people they encountered. In some areas where pigs were introduced, the death toll among the indigenous population was as high as 90 per cent.

The role of pigs as a cultural marker in Spain shouldn't be underestimated and it was the Spaniards who introduced pigs to the New World.

NORTHERN EUROPEAN PIGS

The Spaniards may have introduced pigs to the American south, but others were responsible for porcine immigration from the east and the north. John Cabot was originally from Venice (where he was known as Zuan Chabotto), but it was England he turned to in search of funding for his exploratory expeditions. He travelled to the New World from the north, which brought him to the part of the north-eastern coast known today as New England.

Cabot apparently brought pigs with him on his journey from the UK, at the tail end of the 15th century. When the ship left Bristol harbour it contained a small herd of Celtic pigs, but we don't know much about what actually happened to them. If they survived the journey, de Soto's pigs may not actually have been the first to set hoof on the US mainland.

The first English colony in America was Jamestown, in modern-day Virginia, founded in 1607 by three ships and 100 people. As far as we know, Sir Walter Raleigh had three sows with him. Sources from Jamestown suggest three sows and a boar. In any case, after only 18 months the herd had expanded to 60 pigs. Two years later there were between 500 and 600 pigs roaming the forests and countryside around

«Pork was popular in all the colonies and the pigs' incredible reproductive capacity inevitably led to a pork surplus. This excess meat was salted and stored in barrels filled with brine»

the area – maintaining a precise headcount became impossible. Twenty years later, there were countless pigs – or, at least, so many that nobody could be bothered to count them any more.

The colony was beset by hunger, death and struggle, but was aided by occasional, irregular arrivals of supplies and assistance from England, including pigs. The pigs were mostly left to wander freely and thrived on this half-wild, half-domesticated arrangement. Pigs were the most important animals the first colonists had and they often helped to save the colony from starvation in its early years. Pigs are, however, unruly animals. Just like the Spaniards, the English immigrants struggled with pigs consuming their crops, which also created major problems for the indigenous population. They weren't used to constructing fences strong enough to repel a determined pig, which was bad news for the corn and the natives alike.

Sir Walter Raleigh

Eventually, the trouble the pigs were causing led the colonists to gather them on a single island. This island became known, somewhat inevitably, as 'Hog Island' and the settlers would go there to collect pigs as and when they were needed. The meat from these pigs was often salted and smoked. Some believe that it was the natives who taught the settlers to smoke meat, as they had done with other animals since time immemorial, but it's equally likely that the technique was brought from England, where it was also a common practice by this point.

Pork was popular in all the colonies and the pigs' incredible reproductive capacity inevitably led to a pork surplus. This excess meat was salted and stored in barrels filled with brine, and 'barrelled pork' was exported to the Caribbean islands, where it was sold to the ships crossing the Atlantic. Massachusetts exported mostly barrelled pork, while Virginia became known for exporting bacon – but it's not easy to say what sort of bacon this might have been. The distinction wasn't made until much later.

In the early 18th century pigs became far more important than cows. Beef may have been more sought-after, but pork was far more common as everyday food – around two-thirds of meat consumed was pork. This may be the key to pork's relatively lowly status in the 19th century. Pigs were everywhere in early America. They were a common sight wandering the streets of towns and given that each animal typically weighed between 100kg and 150kg (220lb and 330lb), we're talking about a whole lot of pig.

There were so many pigs in Cincinnati in 1835 that it was given the nickname 'Porkopolis'. It was Cincinnati that first started producing meat on an industrial scale. The location was crucial to this – the city was surrounded by large areas where corn was grown, which made for cheap pig feed. Rivers made it relatively easy to transport cargo, both within the immediate area and as far afield as the Gulf of Mexico.

The city slaughtered 100,000 pigs in 1830; by the 1840s this had increased to 250,000 per year and

UNION PACIFIC CONSTRUCTION TRAIN 1868

was as high as 400,000 before the Civil War broke out in the early 1860s. More than 350 million kg (772 million lb) of salted meat and bacon was exported and a contemporary witness named Frederick Law Olmsted wrote about one day in November 1853 when the streets were so jam-packed with pigs that he couldn't move an inch.

Cincinnati was far from the only city to be taken over by pigs. A Norwegian man named Ole Munch Ræder, sent by the Norwegian authorities to study the American legal system, wrote after walking the streets of New York in 1847 that he'd never seen a town or a country with so many adorable pigs just wandering around, in large herds. In New York they eventually introduced regulations to tackle the problem – the fact that all pigs more than 14 inches (35.5cm) high were required to have a ring in their nose suggests that there was a serious need to establish some sort of control over the pigs in the streets.

From around 1850, Chicago took over as the leading city of the pork industry. The development of the railway changed everything, eliminating the advantage that rivers had previously given to other cities. In 1880 4 million pigs were slaughtered in the city and by 1890 Chicago alone was responsible for a full third of meat production in the USA. The area many refer to as the corn belt in the USA was also known as the 'Hog Belt', comprising Iowa, Illinois, Indiana and parts of Michigan, Ohio, Nebraska, Kansas, Minnesota and Missouri. Where you find corn, you also find pigs, and pork production is still hugely important in this region today.

And this, at last, is where modern bacon enters our story.

BACON
becomes bacon

AT THE END of the 19th century it was still normal for farms to slaughter their own animals. The pieces of meat would typically be salted and stored in barrels before winter arrived and some of them would later be smoked. As James Fenimore Cooper wrote in 1845, 'I hold a family to be in a desperate way when the mother can see the bottom of the pork barrel.' Colloquially, this 'barrelled pork' was different from bacon. Bacon was dry salted, while barrelled pork was salted in brine. The difference lay in the salting technique, rather than the cut of the meat – in theory, bacon could be made using the shoulder, the loin, or any other part of the pig.

With industrialisation came the need to standardise terminology and techniques, to make trading easier. In 1930s' Porkopolis the following classifications were used, graded by quality:

CLEAR PORK – the finest cuts from the barrelled pork, including large sides of meat with the bones removed. This was sold in New England and in other places where 'only the best would do'.

MESS PORK – pork rounds and sides. The Navy was the main purchaser of this.

PRIME PORK – smaller sides, shoulder pieces and jaws. This was sold mainly to boats and Southern markets.

BULK PORK – this could be just about anything, including the head, knuckles and feet. It was sent by boat to Mississippi, where it was probably distributed via New Orleans to slave plantations throughout the Southern states.

«In 1915 the world was first introduced to a machine that could carve thin, fine rashers of bacon.»

These four categories were doubled to eight in 1850, when Chicago took over as the leading producer. This meat was sold simply by category, rather than under a brand name.

To distinguish bacon products from other types of meat, the American traders in the Hog Belt began to use the word 'bacon' exclusively to describe salted (and usually smoked) pork belly. This is the precise moment at which American bacon parted ways with its English counterpart, which is made with meat from the loin, rather than the belly.

The important thing to note is that the industrial producers, unlike farmers, used brine to salt bacon, in a break with the traditional definition of bacon as dry salted. Instead, the specific cut of meat became the deciding factor for whether something qualified as bacon: bacon was made from the belly, whether it had been salted dry or in brine. In other words, the definition of bacon had been turned completely on its head. Why?

Using brine is easier than dry salting. In the USA there's also a long tradition of using sugar during the process (like salt, sugar can be used to draw water out of the meat). Too much sugar and the meat can turn black when fried, as the sugar caramelises. Too little sugar and the taste becomes too salty for the American palate. Salting the meat in brine makes it easier to maintain stable conditions, but many people claim that something is lost in the process. The USA also produced something known as 'fancy bacon', which was made using traditional dry-salting methods.

Bacon and ham ended up in high demand from consumers, at the expense of traditional barrelled pork. Between 1890 and 1900 production of bacon (and ham) increased by 48 per cent, while barrelled-pork production increased by only 9 per cent.

BRANDING ARRIVES

This explosion in production is closely related to the introduction of brand names. The first bacon brands arose in the second half of the 19th century – people no longer bought simply 'bacon', but 'Armour bacon', or some other brand. This allowed producers to charge a higher price for their meat. This development was largely thanks to the lowly status of barrelled pork, which was sold anonymously, without any logos. Bacon, unlike ham, didn't have a particularly high status, but this would all change with the introduction of branding and modern marketing techniques.

Two firms stand out during this period: Armour and Oscar Mayer. These brands still exist today and continue to vie for dominance of the North American market. In the 1920s Armour began advertising 'Star' bacon. This could be eaten not just for breakfast but also for 'fancy luncheon dishes' and 'smart supper menus'.

SLICED BACON AND BACON MARKETING

Marketing was all about establishing a higher status for bacon. This went hand in hand with new slicing techniques, which gave us bacon as we know it today.

There's a limit to how thinly you can slice meat with a knife. Even the sharpest knife is unable to carve anything like the thin, machine-sliced strips we know as bacon. This meant that nobody, prior to this point in history, had eaten anything like the thin, crispy rashers of bacon that dominate today. Previously,

bacon had been bought in large pieces that could be carved into slices at home, or by the butcher. Either way, the carving was always done with a knife.

In 1915 the world was first introduced to a machine that could carve thin, fine rashers of bacon. Put into operation by Armour, initially the machine could cut a dizzying 100 slices in a minute, but by the end of the 1920s this had risen to 300 slices a minute. For more than twenty years, everything else was still done by hand. It wasn't until the late 1940s that almost the entire process would be mechanised.

Selling bacon pre-sliced not only meant that it could be sold for a higher price, but it also began to appeal to a new market, one with considerably greater disposable income. Bacon had finally taken hold with the middle class. The advertisements Armour took out in the *Woman's Home Companion* and *McCall's* were full of pictures of well-dressed, good-looking men and women tucking into their bacon.

The only aspect of our modern, packaged bacon still to be finalised was precisely that – the packaging. Packs of bacon from the 1920s were wrapped in cellophane, which worked well enough by the standards of the time, but was dramatically improved upon with the introduction of vacuum sealing in the 1950s.

Bacon as we know it had finally arrived. It had undergone fundamental changes over the past 100 years, and when a British delegation visited the USA in 1951 they could testify that the bacon there 'bears little or no resemblance' to what the British recognised as bacon.

The pick of the pig

The carcass is first divided in two along the spine, then into front and back halves.

The front is separated from the back with a cut between the 4th and 5th ribs.

WHAT CAN THEY BE USED FOR?

1. HEAD
Boiled fresh, or salted and smoked (mostly used for decoration), turned into head cheese – a jelly-like terrine – or minced.

2. EARS
Pickled, boiled or deep-fried.

3. NECK/COLLAR
A slighty fatty cut that is made into chops, steaks, diced pork and mince or can be deboned, rolled and roasted.

4. SHOULDER
Fatty, flavoursome and forgiving, this cut makes for a fantastic roasting joint or also works well diced and slowly stewed.

5. HOCK
Often smoked and boiled or roasted.

6. TROTTERS
Boiled or braised.

7. LOIN
Used to make back bacon. Can be made into cutlets, or lightly salted and smoked to form sandwich ham, or most often rolled and roasted whole to give brilliant crackling.

8. FILLET
Tender long, lean cut often cooked whole or pan fried as medallions.

9. RIBS
Beautiful marinated and slow-cooked or barbecued.

10. BELLY
Used to make streaky bacon. Often braised or roasted, this cut gives soft flesh, flavoursome fat and crispy crackling.

11. CHUMP
Made into chunky chops and then grilled, fried or barbecued.

12. LEG
Usually roasted whole or made into steaks or escalopes. Also often made into sandwich ham.

13. GAMMON HOCK
Often lightly salted, smoked and boiled to make gammon.

14. TAIL
Pickled or grilled.

«The one point everyone agrees on is that it should be made using pork and salt. Everything else is open for discussion.»

BACON isn't just bacon

YOU'D THINK THAT bacon was just … well, bacon. But things are rarely that simple and, sure enough, the word means very different things in the UK, Canada, the USA and Norway.

There's surprisingly little consensus on how bacon should be made. Should you use pork belly, for example, or are back cuts better? We can't even agree on which part of the animal to use. The one point everyone agrees on is that it should be made using pork and salt. Everything else is open for discussion. Preference is everything.

Different countries sell 'bacon' made from pork ribs, belly, back … even shoulder. Different types of bacon vary wildly. Some are fatty, while others are lean. It can be dry salted, or salted in brine. It's not unusual for sugar to be added, but it's not obligatory either. The Italians like to use seasoning for their pancetta.

In many countries it's generally agreed that bacon should taste smokey. Some use real smoke, but many use 'liquid smoke' flavouring. The smoke can be real or synthetic, but any real fan will spot the difference instantly.

How do you
COOK
your bacon?

There are any number of ways to prepare bacon; here are a few of them.

Pick your favourite!

«*Frying bacon in a pan is fine if you're just cooking a few rashers for breakfast. But it has its limitations.*»

PAN-FRYING BACON

FIRST, YOU NEED to decide what sort of fat you want to fry your bacon in. If the bacon itself isn't fatty enough it can easily burn and stick to the frying pan (unless you use a non-stick pan).

If you decide to use cooking fat, you have a choice between butter and oil. Butter works well, but the disadvantage is that it burns at high temperatures. Burnt butter is an indicator that you're using too high a heat.

Some people don't like the taste of butter-fried bacon, in which case oil is the way to go. Neutral oils like sunflower oil, rapeseed oil, or corn oil will impart the least flavour. Olive oil has a stronger aroma and taste, which most people don't enjoy with bacon.

Finding the right temperature is crucial to getting the right result and to how long it will take. The lower the temperature, the more control you have but, unfortunately, it does take a lot longer.

Frying bacon in a pan is fine if you're just cooking a few rashers for breakfast. But it has its limitations. Once you have five rashers or so of bacon in a pan, you're going to start running out of space. If you're cooking for several people, or making a recipe that calls for more than five rashers of fried bacon, you might to want to get the hang of cooking bacon in the oven if you don't want to cook in batches.

Another method, rarely used, may also be worth trying: frying bacon in water. Starting with both water and bacon in the frying pan, the water will initially boil the bacon, melting away some of the fat. As the water evaporates, the bacon will begin to fry in this fat. Again, it's important not to use too high a temperature. This method offers a more controlled form of frying and may result in slightly crispier bacon – which you prefer is down to personal taste.

COOKING BACON IN THE OVEN

USING AN OVEN gives you most control when cooking lots of bacon at once. If you have so much bacon that it needs to be divided into multiple batches in the frying pan, it'll be a lot quicker to use the oven.

The simplest technique is simply to cover an oven tray with baking paper and lay out the bacon on top of it. It doesn't matter if the rashers are pressed right up against each other – bacon shrinks during cooking, so the rashers will separate nicely. With an oven preheated to 200°C/400°F/Gas Mark 6, it should take around 12–13 minutes, but all ovens vary slightly. I like to set a timer for 12 minutes, then check how the bacon is doing when the time is up. If it needs more time I let it cook a little longer, checking it once a minute. It doesn't take long to get the hang of this method and you'll soon figure out how long it takes to give you exactly the bacon you prefer.

If you want to collect the liquid bacon fat, it's easy to pour it from the baking tray – easier than from a frying pan, in fact.

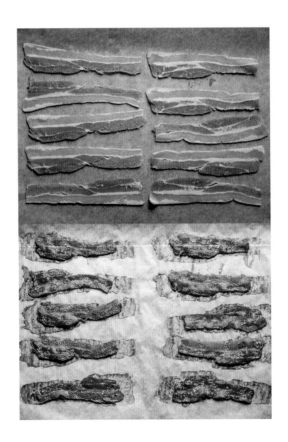

«Barbecuing can be worth the effort, but you shouldn't take your eyes off the bacon for a second throughout the process.»

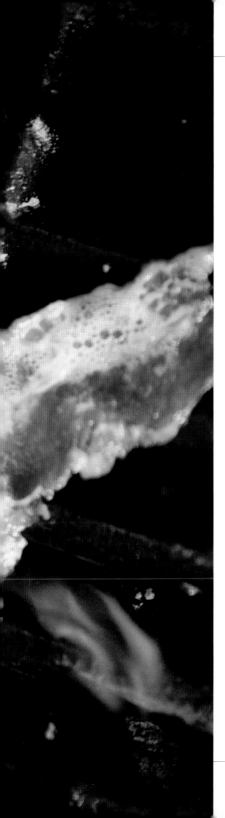

BARBECUING BACON

A BARBECUE IS often less than ideal for frying bacon, just because of how burning hot it can get. It can be worth the effort, but you shouldn't take your eyes off the bacon for a second throughout the process.

It's always worth remembering to set up two heat zones on a barbecue – one hot and one 'cold'.

If you're using a gas-powered barbecue with multiple burners, you can leave one (or two) of them off. This forms a 'cold' zone where you can grill over indirect heat, which is clearly the best way to cook bacon on a barbecue.

COOKING BACON IN A WAFFLE IRON

A WAFFLE IRON is a surprisingly useful instrument for frying bacon. Both the temperature and the non-stick coating are perfectly suited to the task and can definitely be recommended.

The problem is cleaning it afterwards. Unless you like your waffles with a distinctly bacon-y flavour, you're going to need to clean it very thoroughly indeed.

COOKING BACON IN A MICROWAVE

COOKING BACON IN a microwave works surprisingly well if you're looking to cook only a few rashers. Line a plate with some kitchen paper, preferably two or three layers, then lay three or four rashers of bacon on top.

Microwaving at full power (800–1,000 watts), it will take around three minutes to cook three rashers. Feel free to experiment – the cooking time varies depending on the oven and the type of bacon.

«Cooking bacon in a microwave works surprisingly well.»

RECIPES

The recipes in this book are a mix of old and new favourites selected from the culinary world of bacon. They're all simple to make – you won't need any fancy equipment or knowledge of molecular gastronomy (don't ask…). Some of the recipes can be thrown together in 5 minutes, while others will require a little more time and effort. I promise, they're all worth it!

Most of the recipes are tailored to one or two people, but you'll notice a few that are quite a bit more substantial. The main goal is that they should all be simple to make, whether you're at home alone for the evening, or if you're looking to share your love of bacon with those around you.

A quick note regarding portion sizes: if I write '5 rashers of bacon', you should always feel free to double it. Have you ever heard of anyone complaining about too much bacon in, say, a pasta carbonara? Of course not. Neither have I. The rule is simple: if in doubt, too much bacon is better than not enough!

The bacon used in these recipes is always smoked, unless otherwise specified.

Christopher

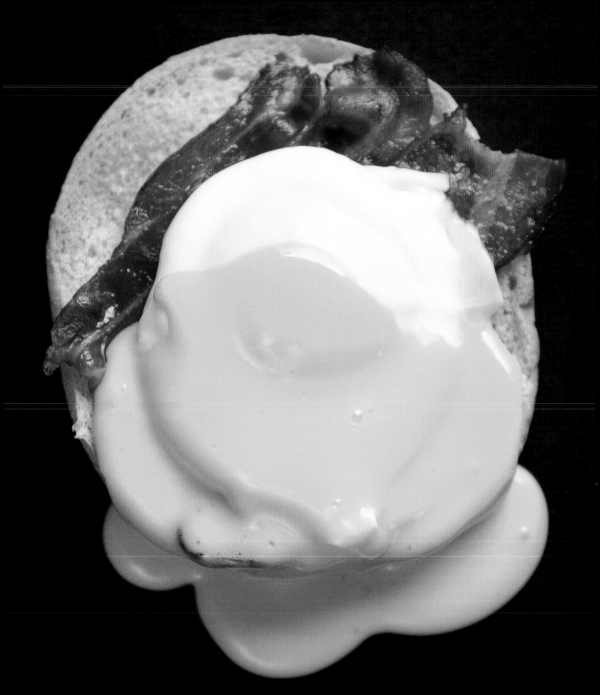

EGGS BENEDICT

A morning-after recipe so good it's worth the hangover.

SERVES 1

4 RASHERS OF STREAKY OR BACK BACON
1 BRIOCHE BUN OR ENGLISH MUFFIN
3 EGGS
150g (5oz) BUTTER
1 LEMON WEDGE
CAYENNE PEPPER

Fry the bacon in a dry pan until crispy. Toast the muffin or brioche in a toaster or in the oven. Poach one of the eggs – bring a pan of water to the boil, then turn off the heat. Crack 1 egg into a cup, then tip carefully into the hot water and leave it undisturbed for 4 minutes.

To make the Hollandaise the sauce, melt the butter. Separate the yolks and whites of the 2 remaining eggs (you'll only need the yolks). Whisk the yolks in a heatproof bowl, then place the bowl over a pan half-filled with boiling hot water. Gradually add the melted butter to the bowl, whisking constantly. Add the lemon juice and a pinch of cayenne pepper to taste.

Serve the bacon on the bread with a poached egg on top and coat with plenty of sauce.

Match made in New York

AFTER A NIGHT on the town in 1894, a man staggered to the breakfast table at the Waldorf Astoria Hotel in New York, feeling distinctly the worse for wear. When the waiter arrived, the man couldn't stomach anything on the menu, so he just ordered exactly what he wanted: toast, poached egg, a dollop of hollandaise sauce and bacon.

When the legendary maître d'hôtel, Oscar Tschirky, received the order, he was so impressed by the combination that he rushed out to greet the customer who had ordered it. He was called Lemuel Benedict and when his breakfast creation ended up on the hotel menu, he was immortalised in the name of the dish: Eggs Benedict.

BITE-SIZE BACON AND EGG CUPS

Stick these in the oven while you're taking a shower.

SERVES 2
2 RASHERS OF STREAKY BACON
OIL, FOR GREASING
1 EGG
2 TBSP GRATED CHEDDAR CHEESE
1 TBSP CHOPPED CHIVES
BREAD, BUTTER AND SLICED TOMATO, TO SERVE

Preheat the oven to 180°C/350°F/Gas Mark 4. Cut each rasher of bacon in two, then lay two strips across each other in the greased cup of a muffin tin. Repeat with the remaining two slices. The bacon should hang slightly over the sides of the cups.

In a clean bowl, whisk the egg with the cheese and chives. Pour the resulting mixture into the muffin cups and bake in the oven for 10–15 minutes until they rise.

Serve with bread, butter and sliced tomato.

Irresistible chemistry

RESEARCHERS AT NEWCASTLE University have discovered that the chemical reaction that takes place when you fry bacon produces an almost irresistible combination of smell and flavour. I know, I know ... 'anyone could have told you that'. But there's some surprisingly complex chemistry behind it. The reaction between the amino acids that make up the protein in bacon and the sugar in the fat results in an explosion of hundreds of scents and flavours powerful enough to make even vegetarians struggle with their principles. What can you do? It's hard to argue with chemistry.

«I love super crispy, almost burned, snapping-crispy bacon.»

DAVID LYNCH, American film director

EGG EN COCOTTE WITH BACON

Because just calling it 'bacon and eggs in a bowl' wouldn't sound fancy enough.

SERVES 1

2 RASHERS OF BACK OR STREAKY BACON
  (PREFERABLY THICK-CUT)
8 SPINACH LEAVES
1 TSP DICED RED ONION
2 TBSP CRÈME FRAÎCHE
1 EGG
1 TSP CHOPPED CHIVES
SEA SALT FLAKES

Preheat the oven to 180°C/350°F/Gas Mark 4. Line a baking tray with baking paper. Lay the bacon slices out on the tray and bake for 7–8 minutes.

Place the spinach leaves and onion in a small ovenproof dish. Add the crème fraîche, then line the sides of the dish with the bacon. Break the egg into the dish and bake in the oven for 12–15 minutes.

Serve with chopped chives and a little salt.

Bringing home the bacon

THERE ARE SEVERAL different theories about where the phrase 'to bring home the bacon', meaning 'to earn money', comes from. Some claim that it stems from an old form of entertainment at markets, where the aim was to catch and hold on to a slippery greased pig. The winner got to keep the pig, thus literally 'bringing home the bacon'.

Another version dates back to England in the 1100s and the small village of Great Dunmow, where couples who had been married for a year and a day could attempt to swear in front of God and the congregation that they had neither regretted the decision nor argued in all that time. Those who could successfully convince the congregation of their sincerity were given a side

(a 'flitch') of bacon to take home with them.

These 'Dunmow Flitch Trials' are still held every four years, so any couple who has been married for a year and a day can present themselves in front of a judge and jury, and under cross-examination try to persuade the 'court' of their unsullied happiness. Sounds like a high price to pay for a piece of bacon ...

«*Wakey wakey, eggs and bakey.*»
BUDD, *Kill Bill: Volume 2*

BACON AND EGG MUFFINS

You can't serve less than three to anyone.

SERVES 1
3 SLICES OF WHITE BREAD
OIL, FOR GREASING
3 RASHERS OF BACK OR STREAKY BACON
3 EGGS
3 TSP CHOPPED CHIVES

Preheat the oven to 200ºC/400ºF/Gas Mark 6.

Using an upturned glass, cut a circle out of each slice of bread. Brush with a little oil and press down into three cups of a muffin tin. Line the sides of each cup with a rasher of bacon and break an egg into each. Bake in the oven for approximately 20 minutes until the bacon and egg are cooked through. Garnish with chives before serving.

DEVILLED EGGS WITH BACON

A good way to work bacon and eggs into a cold meal.

SERVES 2 AS A SNACK

3 RASHERS OF BACK OR STREAKY BACON
3 EGGS
3 TBSP MAYONNAISE
1 TSP MILD MUSTARD
2 TBSP CHOPPED CHIVES
1 LEMON WEDGE

Preheat the oven to 200°C/400°F/Gas Mark 6. Line a baking tray with baking paper.

Lay the bacon slices out on the tray and bake for approximately 12 minutes. Remove the bacon from the oven and, once it has cooled down, cut into small pieces. Reserve the fat in the tray.

Boil the eggs for 10 minutes, then place them in cold water. Peel off the shell and slice them in half. Remove the yolks and place in a bowl and put the whites to one side. Add the mayonnaise, mustard and chives to the egg yolks. Pour a few tablespoons of the reserved bacon fat into the bowl, squeeze in the lemon juice and stir everything together to form a smooth mixture. Fill the egg whites with this mixture and top with the pieces of bacon to serve.

Bacon on a stick

THE CALIFORNIA-BASED COMPANY Lollyphile specialises in what might politely be termed 'unusual' lollipop flavours, including beer, Chardonnay and breakfast cereal. Naturally, they also have a few variants for bacon lovers –

one chocolate and bacon flavour and another with maple syrup and bacon. As one delighted customer wrote: 'Jesus got my letter!'

NOTE: LOLLYPHILE ALSO sell breast-milk lollipops, so this can go either way …

SOURCE: LOLLYPHILE.COM

BACON TAPENADE

Pure delight in a jar.

SERVES 2 AS A SNACK

5 RASHERS OF BACK OR
  STREAKY BACON
OIL, FOR FRYING
1 GARLIC CLOVE, PEELED
  AND ROUGHLY CHOPPED
2 TBSP CAPERS
200G (7OZ) PITTED OLIVES
2 SUN-DRIED TOMATOES
1 ANCHOVY FILLET
TOAST, TO SERVE

Fry the bacon in the oil until crispy, then
chop into small pieces. Whizz the garlic,
capers, olives, sun-dried tomatoes and
the anchovy in a food processor. Tip
the mixture into a bowl, then stir in the
bacon. Spread it on toast. Pour yourself
a beer. Enjoy.

PAIN AU BACON

The French would have invented this ages ago, if only they'd had decent bacon.

MAKES 3

3 RASHERS OF BACK OR STREAKY BACON
1 SHEET OF PUFF PASTRY
1 EGG, BEATEN (OR 1 EGG YOLK)

Preheat the oven to 200°C/400°F/Gas Mark 6. Line a baking tray with baking paper.
Lay the bacon slices out on the tray and bake for 8–10 minutes until almost crispy.
Cut the pastry into three triangles. With the points facing you, lay a rasher of bacon along the rear edge of each triangle and roll the pastry around the bacon. Brush with the whisked egg or just the yolk and bake for 15–20 minutes until golden brown.

The delicate scent of bacon

BACON COLOGNE was first introduced in 1920, when a French butcher named John Fargginay accidentally combined 11 popular oils that all contained a hint of bacon and the smell was quite recognisable. It was sold in both a mild and a somewhat stronger version, still available today. Combine it with bacon-scented toothpaste, mouthwash and lip balm, and you're all ready for a big date.

SOURCES: FARGINAY.COM, GOODREADS.COM

BACON PROFITEROLES

Cheesy bacon pastry bites – what's not to like?

MAKES APPROXIMATELY 15
15 RASHERS OF BACON OR 225G/8oz BACON BITS
250ML (9FL OZ) WATER
80G (GENEROUS 3oz) BUTTER
100G (3½oz) PLAIN FLOUR
4 EGGS
150G (5oz) GRATED CHEDDAR CHEESE

Preheat the oven to 200°C/400°F/Gas Mark 6. Line a baking tray with baking paper.

Spread the bacon rashers out on the tray and bake for approximately 12 minutes or until the bacon is nice and golden, or if using the bacon pieces fry in a dry pan. Remove the bacon from the oven and, once it has cooled down, chop into small pieces.

Boil the water and butter in a saucepan. Add the cooked bacon and the flour, and stir well, then beat in the eggs, one by one, ensuring each egg has been thoroughly mixed into the dough before adding the next. Stir in the grated cheese.

Use two tablespoons to form the dough into 15 balls, as evenly as you can (each ball should be about the size of a golf ball) and place on the baking tray. They will spread out, so make sure there's plenty of space around each of them. Bake in the oven for 20–25 minutes until lightly golden.

Electrobacon

BACON IS THE title of a 2009 album by Danish electronica artist Mikkel Meyer. The album is inspired by Meyers' grandmother's recipe book and includes songs such as 'Banana split', 'Cheese tart' and, not least, the final track, 'Strawberry cake'. It's enough to make you hungry for more.

BACON JAM

I urge you to try!

MAKES 1 JAR

12 RASHERS OF BACK OR STREAKY
   BACON (OR 175G/6oz BACON BITS)
2 ONIONS, PEELED AND SLICED
3 GARLIC CLOVES, PEELED AND CRUSHED
2 TBSP BROWN SUGAR
50ML (2FL OZ) MAPLE SYRUP
100ML (3½FL OZ) APPLE CIDER VINEGAR
1 CUP OF COFFEE
FRESHLY GROUND BLACK PEPPER
BREAD AND BRIE, TO SERVE

Preheat the oven to 200°C/400°F/Gas Mark 6.
Line a baking tray with baking paper.

Spread the bacon rashers out on the tray and
bake for approximately 12 minutes or until the
bacon is nice and golden, or cook the bacon
pieces in a dry pan. Remove the bacon from
the oven and, once it has cooled down, chop
into small pieces and lay it out on a sheet of
baking paper. Pour off most of the fat from the
pan or tray.

Fry the onions and garlic in the fat in a
pan on a low heat, stirring constantly, until
golden brown.

Combine the brown sugar, syrup, vinegar and
coffee in a bowl, then pour into the pan over
the onions and garlic and leave to cook for a few
minutes, until it reduces and develops a thick
and even consistency. Stir in the bacon. Blend
with a hand-held blender until you think it looks
good (not too thick, not too thin), add a grin-
ding of pepper.

This works particularly well on a slice of
crusty bread with brie. Store in the fridge
and eat before the bacon's expiry date.

BACON BUTTER

If you like garlic butter, you're going to love bacon butter.

MAKES 1 BLOCK
10 RASHERS OF BACK OR
   STREAKY BACON
4 TBSP FRESHLY CHOPPED SAGE
   (OR SOME OTHER SUITABLE HERB)
1 GARLIC CLOVE, PEELED AND
   CRUSHED
150G (5OZ) BUTTER, AT ROOM
   TEMPERATURE
2 TBSP SOURED CREAM

Preheat the oven to 200°C/400°F/Gas Mark 6. Line a baking tray with baking paper.

Spread the bacon out on the tray and bake for approximately 12 minutes or until the bacon is nice and golden. Remove the bacon from the oven and, once it has cooled down, chop into small pieces.

Combine the chopped bacon, sage, garlic, butter and soured cream in a bowl. Pour the resulting mix on to baking paper and shape it into a sausage. Roll it up and place in the fridge.

There aren't many things bacon butter isn't good for. You can use it to fry meat or fish, or lay a few thin slices on hot roast beef and let it melt and run down over the meat before serving. It's also OK to spread it on your bread. Store in the fridge and eat before the bacon's expiry date.

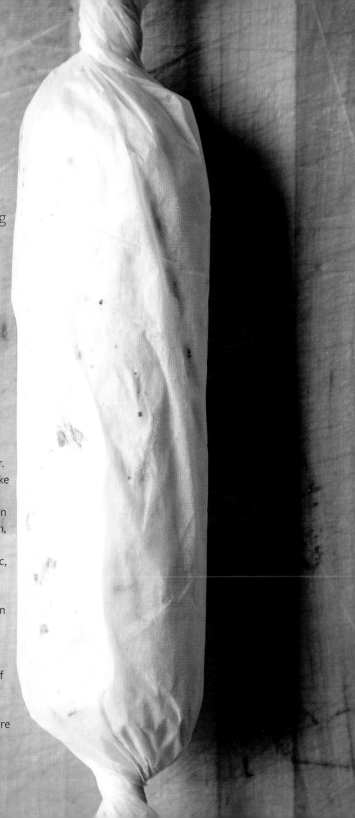

BACONNAISE

My main complaint about mayonnaise: it doesn't taste of bacon.

MAKES 1 JAR
8 RASHERS OF BACK OR STREAKY BACON
1 EGG
100ML (3½FL OZ) SUNFLOWER OIL
LEMON JUICE
SALT AND FRESHLY GROUND BLACK PEPPER

Preheat the oven to 200°C/400°F/Gas Mark 6. Place the bacon on a grilling rack with a tray underneath, to catch the dripping fat, and bake until crispy, approximately 12 minutes. Leave the fat to cool a little.

Break the egg into a cylindrical container, suitable for use with a hand-held blender. Add the oil, lemon juice and salt and pepper to taste and combine using the blender. Add the reserved bacon fat gradually as you blend the mixture.

Crumble the crispy bacon into small pieces and stir into the mayonnaise. Store in the fridge and eat before the bacon's expiry date.

Arnold

ARNOLD SCHWARZENEGGER IS well known for his one-liners in his movies, but he's not bad at them offscreen either. When he was hit by an egg thrown by a protester at a political event, Arnold made the following comment: 'This guy owes me bacon now. I mean there's no two ways about it … you can't just have eggs without bacon.'

«Pork chops and bacon, my two favourite animals.»
HOMER, *The Simpsons*

BACON-WRAPPED GRILLED CHEESE

SEE RECIPE, OVERLEAF »

BACON-WRAPPED GRILLED CHEESE

A classic home-alone snack.

MAKES 2 SLICES
1 TBSP MILD MUSTARD
2 SLICES OF SOFT WHITE BREAD
2 TBSP GRATED CHEDDAR CHEESE
6 RASHERS OF BACK OR STREAKY BACON
BUTTER, FOR FRYING

Spread half the mustard on each slice of bread. Sprinkle the cheese on top of one slice, then place the other slice, mustard-side down, on top. Wrap the whole thing in bacon – try to get it as tight and even as possible.

Fry the wrapped sandwich in a little butter in a frying pan until the bacon is golden. Use a lid on the pan if you're not sure that the cheese is melting properly.

Your bacon or your life!

IN MARCH 2014 a McDonald's restaurant in the USA experienced a real-life *Falling Down* situation. Just like Michael Douglas in the 1993 film, 30-year-old Shaneka Monique Torres opened fire in a fast-food restaurant because the burger she was served didn't look like it did in the photograph. The bacon-obsessed woman had ordered a cheeseburger with bacon from the drive-thru, but when it arrived, it was without bacon. When she complained, she was offered a free replacement as compensation, but when she came back to collect the food, the bacon was missing once again. Apparently, this was enough to tip her over the edge, because she drew a gun and fired several shots at the restaurant. Clearly, this is a woman who really, really loves her bacon.

Nobody was injured, but she received a 3–7-year prison sentence. Presumably without access to bacon.

SOURCE: NTB.NO

BACON CROQUE-MONSIEUR

The world's greatest sandwich just got even better.

MAKES 1

2 RASHERS OF BACK OR STREAKY BACON
  (PREFERABLY THICK-CUT)
BUTTER FOR SPREADING
2 SLICES OF SOFT WHITE BREAD
1 TSP MILD MUSTARD
2 TBSP GRATED CHEESE

Fry the bacon in a dry pan the way you like it. Spread butter on both slices of bread and place one of them butter-side down in a frying pan. Spread mustard on the top side and place the bacon on top. Sprinkle the cheese over the bacon, then put the other slice of bread on top, butter-side up. Fry on a medium heat until the underside is golden.

Turn the sandwich over, so the other buttered slice is face down, and place a lid on the pan (to ensure the cheese melts). When the underside is also golden and toasted, your sandwich is ready. Slice in half and enjoy.

Bacon Vs sex

WHEN THE CANADIAN packaged-meats company Maple Leaf Foods did a rough survey, they found that 43 per cent of those surveyed would rather eat bacon than have sex, 23 per cent of men ranked bacon as their favourite smell; and 23 per cent thought that their partners loved bacon more than them.

SOURCE: MAPLE LEAF FOODS

BACON FINGERS

Finally, a dish where you can use your fingers with impunity!

MAKES 10 FINGERS

400G (14OZ) STRONG FLOUR
1 TSP SALT
150ML (5FL OZ) WATER
2 TSP DRIED YEAST
1 TBSP OIL, PLUS EXTRA FOR GREASING
10 RASHERS OF STREAKY BACON
10 BLACK PEPPERCORNS
4 TBSP BROWN SUGAR

Mix the flour, salt, water, yeast and oil together and form into a dough. Put into a lightly oiled bowl, cover with a damp cloth and leave to rise in a warm place for 1 hour until doubled in size.

Preheat the oven to 180°C/350°F/Gas Mark 4. Line a baking tray with baking paper.

Give the dough a quick knead then form it into 10 sausages and wrap a rasher of bacon around each one.

Grind the peppercorns and combine them with the sugar. Dip the bacon fingers in this powder, making sure as much sugar and pepper sticks to them as possible. Place the fingers on the tray and cook in the oven until the cooked through.

Bacon shop

IT'S ASTONISHING (AND a little disturbing) how many websites are dedicated to bacon. You can find everything from recipes to largely useless bacon trivia, and there are almost no products out there that you can't buy in a bacon-ified version.

The largest selection is probably found on amazon.com, where you can buy almost anything: bacon soda, bacon chocolate, bacon coffee, bacon makeup, bacon

Christmas decorations, bacon costumes (even for dogs!), bacon Monopoly, bacon plasters ... somebody stop me! And if you aren't quite ready to make a lifelong declaration of your love of bacon, there are always bacon-themed temporary tattoos ...

SOURCE: AMAZON.COM

«Mmmm ... unexplained bacon.»
HOMER, *The Simpsons*

CHEESY BREAD WITH BACON

For something that tastes so good, this is surprisingly easy to make.

MAKES 2

400G (14OZ) STRONG BREAD FLOUR
150ML (5FL OZ) WATER
2 TBSP OIL, PLUS EXTRA FOR GREASING
1 TSP SEA SALT
½ TSP DRIED YEAST
10 RASHERS OF BACK OR STREAKY BACON
200G (7OZ) GRATED CHEDDAR CHEESE

Mix the flour, water, oil, salt and yeast together to form a dough. Put into a lightly oiled bowl, cover with a damp cloth and leave to rise in a warm place for 1 hour (or overnight in the fridge) until doubled in size.

Preheat the oven to 200°C/400°F/Gas Mark 6. Line a baking tray with baking paper.

Spread the bacon out on the tray and bake until it's nice and crispy, approximately 12 minutes. Set aside.

Turn the oven to the maximum heat.

Give the dough a quick knead then split the dough into two pieces and roll out as thinly as possible (either square, oblong or round). Spread half the grated cheese and bacon over one side of one of the dough pieces, then fold the other side over. Repeat with the remaining piece of dough.

Place the dough on a baking tray and bake in the oven at maximum heat for approximately 10 minutes – pay attention throughout and take them out when the dough looks nice and brown. Either divide into smaller pieces, or just eat whole.

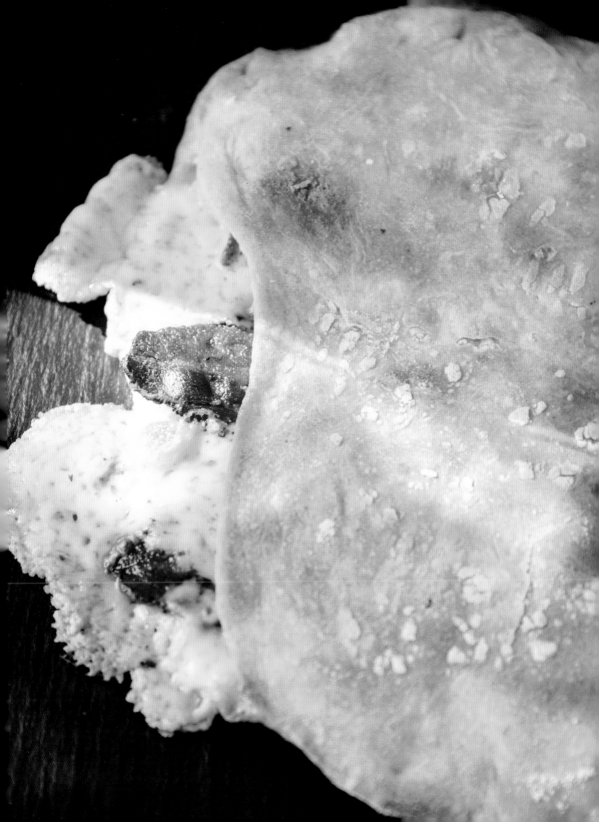

SCRAMBLED EGGS, MUSHROOMS AND BACON ON TOAST

You won't have tasted better scrambled eggs.

MAKES 1
4 RASHERS OF BACK OR STREAKY BACON
2 BUTTON MUSHROOMS, CHOPPED
1 SLICE OF SOFT WHITE BREAD
1 GARLIC CLOVE, PEELED AND HALVED
A LITTLE BUTTER (OPTIONAL)
2 EGGS
2 TBSP RICOTTA CHEESE
SALT

Cook the bacon in a frying pan to your own preference then set aside. Fry the mushrooms in the bacon fat until cooked. Toast the bread, then rub one side with the garlic clove. Rub it in thoroughly, to give the bread a nice garlicky taste, then top with the mushrooms.

Add a little butter to the frying pan, if you like, then whisk the eggs and pour them into the pan. Add the ricotta and stir constantly, then remove the pan from the heat before the eggs are completely finished cooking. The heat from the pan will finish the job in a few seconds. Add salt to taste. Spread the scrambled eggs over the mushrooms and top the whole thing off with the fried bacon. Enjoy!

BACON BURGER

This avoids the classic bacon burger mistake –
not enough bacon.

MAKES 1

150G (5OZ) BEEF MINCE
TABASCO SAUCE
8 RASHERS OF BACK OR STREAKY BACON
OIL, FOR FRYING
2 TBSP KETCHUP
2 TBSP MUSTARD
2 TBSP MAYONNAISE
1 BURGER BUN
2 SLICES OF CHEDDAR CHEESE
LETTUCE LEAVES
2 SLICES OF TOMATO
FRESHLY GROUND BLACK PEPPER

Mix the mince with a little pepper and a few drops of Tabasco and form into a burger patty. Wrap it carefully with bacon, enough to completely cover the top of the burger. Fry the burger bacon-side down in a frying pan with a little oil, until the burger and bacon are cooked to your liking. Turn it over and fry for another 2–3 minutes on a high heat.

To make the dressing, mix the ketchup, mustard and mayonnaise in a small bowl. Toast the bun. Deck the bottom half with the cheese, lettuce, tomato slices and some of the dressing, then top with the burger and drizzle with a little more of the dressing before placing the other half of the bun on top.

First and biggest

AMERICAN FAST FOOD chain A&W Restaurants proudly claim to be the first fast-food restaurant to have added bacon to a cheeseburger. The largest cheese and bacon burger ever made was in Carlton, Minnesota, and weighed 914kg (2,015lb), had a 3-metre (10-ft) diameter and was topped with 27kg (59½ lb) of bacon!

BEER CAN BURGER

You're going to need a cold beer and a barbecue with a lid. Doesn't sound like a bad start ...

MAKES 1 BURGER

½ ONION, PEELED AND FINELY CHOPPED
200G (7OZ) BEEF MINCE
475ML (17FL OZ) CAN OF COLD BEER
5 RASHERS OF BACK OR STREAKY BACON
 (PREFERABLY THICK-CUT)
2 CHERRY TOMATOES
A FEW MUSHROOMS
A HANDFUL OF GRATED CHEDDAR CHEESE
SALT AND FRESHLY GROUND BLACK PEPPER

Preheat the barbecue.

Mix the onion with the mince and season with salt and pepper. Pack this tightly around the can of beer, to about halfway up (see overleaf). Wrap the bacon around the mince. Loosen the meat carefully and remove the beer can, to form a 'cup'. Fill it with tomatoes, mushrooms, or anything else you like. Sprinkle the cheese on top, pushing it down into the cup.

Place on the grill and close the lid. Don't grill it over direct heat – it could burn. This can also easily be done in the oven, at 200ºC/400ºF/Gas Mark 6. In either case, the burger will be finished when the bacon looks nice and golden.
IMPORTANT! While the burger is cooking, open the beer and drink it.

HOW TO MAKE A BEER CAN BURGER

BACON-COVERED TOAST

Better to top your toast with a wall-to-wall carpeting of bacon than with a wall-to-wall carpet.

SERVES 1

6 RASHERS OF STREAKY BACON
1 SLICE OF SOFT WHITE BREAD

Weave the bacon into a lattice (see instructions on pages 110-111). Fry the bacon lattice in a dry frying pan until golden on both sides.

Toast the bread (or quickly fry it in the bacon fat). Lay the bacon on top of the bread and you're done.

TIP!
- Serve it with a fried or poached egg.

Bling butty

YOU THINK BUYING someone a bacon sandwich would make for a pretty cheap date? Think again. At Tangberry's coffee house in Cheltenham Gloucestershire, at least.

The Bacon Bling sandwich cost a dizzying £150 – making it, naturally, the world's most expensive bacon sandwich. Is it made of pure gold? I hear you say. And, yes, it is! As well as seven rashers of bacon from a rare pedigree pig, truffles, truffle oil, watercress, saffron and eggs from free-range hens, it actually contains edible gold leaf.

It took about 15 minutes to create this marvel, and the profits went to charity. This might have been a mistake, given that the café is now closed ...

SOURCES: DAILYMAIL.CO.UK, WORLDRECORDACADEMY.COM

BACON BREAD

Perfect hiking food: scoop out the centre of a loaf of bread and fill it with bacon and other goodies!

SERVES 6

12 RASHERS OF BACK OR STREAKY BACON
½ A BUTTERNUT SQUASH
OIL, FOR GREASING
1 LOAF OF CRUSTY BREAD
5 TBSP TAPENADE (SEE TIPS!)
5 PICKLED GREEN OR RED PEPPERS
2 BALLS OF MOZZARELLA, CUT INTO SLICES

Preheat the oven to 200°C/400°F/Gas Mark 6. Line a baking tray with baking paper. Lay the bacon slices out on the tray and bake until golden, approximately 12 minutes.

Cut the squash into slices and grill or fry them in a little oil until softened and golden. Cut off the top of the bread lengthways. Scoop out the insides (these can be dried and used for something else). Spread the tapenade on the inside of the bread, covering the bottom and a long way up the sides. Layer the fillings in the order of your choice: for example, pepper, mozzarella, bacon, squash, mozzarella and bacon to finish. Replace the lid.

Take this with you to a picnic, or to the beach!

TIPS!

- You can make your own tapenade by blending olives, sun-dried tomatoes, capers and an anchovy into a paste.

- It can be worth slicing the filled loaf before taking it with you, but it's not essential.

AVOCADO BACON

Everyone likes vegetables when they're served with bacon.

SERVES 2

10 RASHERS OF BACK OR STREAKY BACON
50G (2OZ) PEAS
2 AVOCADOS
4 TBSP FETA CHEESE CUBES
1 LEMON WEDGE
SALT AND FRESHLY GROUND BLACK PEPPER

Preheat the oven to 200°C/400°F/Gas Mark 6.

Line a baking tray with baking paper. Lay the bacon slices out on the tray and bake for approximately 12 minutes. Once it has cooled down, chop the bacon into small pieces.

Boil the peas for 1 minute, then drain. Cut each avocado in two, remove the stone and scrape out the flesh. Put the avocado shells to one side.

Blend the avocado flesh, half the bacon, the feta cheese and the peas together with a hand-held blender. Season with lemon juice, salt and pepper. Spoon the mixture back into the avocado shells and garnish with the rest of the bacon.

Liquid bacon

IT WAS ONLY a matter of time. Two of life's greatest pleasures, beer and bacon, were inevitably going to end up being combined to make bacon beer. To this end, the American brewery Rogue Ales, in Oregon, has come up with Voodoo Doughnut Bacon Maple Ale. Sadly, they don't export much of it even within the USA, let alone abroad, so the best way to taste this liquid gold is to visit one of the brewery's many bars, mostly located in Oregon. The bars are even dog-friendly, with their own dog menu!

If you're after something a little stronger, perhaps Bakon Vodka is the drink for you? The American company Black Rock Spirits tested recipes for more than two years before settling on this potato-based bacon elixir.

Otherwise, maybe we could tempt you to a bacon martini, with blue-cheese-stuffed olives?

SOURCES: ROGUE.COM, BAKONVODKA.COM

BACON AND POTATO CAKE WITH CHEESE

SEE RECIPE, OVERLEAF »

BACON AND POTATO CAKE WITH CHEESE

The joy of using so much bacon in a single dish is indescribable.

SERVES 4 HUNGRY PEOPLE AS A SIDE

OIL, FOR GREASING
AT LEAST 3 PACKS OF BACK OR STREAKY BACON
6 POTATOES, WASHED AND PEELED, IF YOU LIKE
150G (5OZ) CHEDDAR CHEESE, GRATED
SALT AND FRESHLY GROUND BLACK PEPPER

Preheat the oven to 180°C/350°F/Gas Mark 4.

Cut a circle out of some baking paper, as big as your largest ovenproof frying pan. Brush a little oil over the inside of the frying pan and lay the paper on top. Lay the bacon slices on the paper, from the middle of the pan and out towards the edges, overlapping them a bit. To avoid a great big lump of bacon in the middle, only position every other slice all the way in. Every other slice should start 2–3cm (¾–1¼ in) from the centre and overlap the edge of the pan.

When the whole pan is covered with bacon, cut the potatoes into slices. Cover the bacon with a layer of potato, sprinkle with salt and pepper and cover with some of the cheese. Continue adding layers of potatoes, cheese, salt and pepper, ending with the remaining potatoes to form the shape of a mountain. Fold the overhanging rashers of bacon over the top and cover with a small lid (so the bacon doesn't curl up). Cook in the oven for 2½ hours until cooked through. Cover with foil if the bacon starts to get too dark.

FRISÉE SALAD WITH BACON

The perfect lunch for a lazy day.

SERVES 1, AS A LUNCH
4 RASHERS OF BACK OR STREAKY BACON (PREFERABLY THICK CUT)
1 SHALLOT, PEELED AND FINELY CHOPPED
1 TSP DIJON MUSTARD
5 TBSP OLIVE OIL
2 TBSP LEMON JUICE
5 LEAVES OF FRISÉE
2 EGGS
SALT AND FRESHLY GROUND BLACK PEPPER

Fry the bacon in a frying pan until crispy. Put the shallot and mustard in a large bowl and whisk together, gradually adding the olive oil as you whisk. Season to taste with lemon juice, salt and pepper.

Wash the lettuce thoroughly and dry. Using your hands, stir the leaves into the dressing, making sure they're nicely covered. Put them on a serving plate.

Bring some water in a saucepan to the boil, then take off the heat. Break the eggs, one at a time, into a cup. Pour them carefully into the boiling-temperature water and leave for 4 minutes. Using a slotted spoon, lift the eggs out and put on kitchen paper to drain. Put the poached eggs on top of the lettuce leaves, along with the crispy bacon.

Live longer with bacon

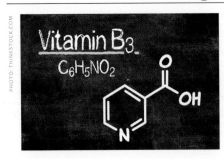

RESEARCHERS HAVE DISCOVERED that vitamin B_3, found in foods such as peanuts, sun-dried tomatoes and, naturally, bacon, can extend your life.

The research was carried out on worms, and those that received large amounts of B_3 lived 10 per cent longer than those that didn't. You probably shouldn't try a bacon-only diet to get your dose of B_3, but it's not a bad excuse ...

SOURCE: HUFFINGTONPOST.COM

BACON PÂTÉ

If you don't like this, you're beyond hope.

SERVES 10

20 RASHERS OF BACK OR STREAKY BACON
5 TBSP COGNAC
3 TBSP BUTTER
1 ONION, PEELED AND CHOPPED
3 GARLIC CLOVES, PEELED AND MINCED
600G (1LB 7OZ) MINCE, PREFERABLY PORK
1 TSP DRIED THYME
1 TSP SALT
2 EGGS
100ml (3½ FL OZ) DOUBLE CREAM
FRESHLY GROUND BLACK PEPPER

Preheat the oven to 180ºC/350ºF/Gas Mark 4. Lay the bacon side by side in a terrine or loaf tin just slightly overlapping, and let the bacon hang over the edges (so you can fold them over the pâté at the end). Grill any remaining bacon until crispy.

Pour the cognac into a pan and heat until almost all of it has evaporated. Add the butter, onion and garlic and fry on a medium heat for about 10 minutes. Mix the contents of the pan with the mince, in a bowl. Add the thyme, plus the salt and some pepper to taste. Quickly whisk the eggs and add them to the bowl. Add the cream and knead it all together into a smooth mixture.

Add the contents of the pan to the bacon-lined terrine or tin and fold the bacon in over the meat. Put the terrine or loaf tin into a larger roasting tin and pour water into the outer tray until it's approximately two-thirds full. Put in the oven and cook for around 3 hours. If the bacon looks like it might be about to burn, cover with foil. Remove from the oven and leave to cool.

If you're unmoulding the pâté on to a plate, stand the terrine or tin in warm water for a few minutes, to keep it from sticking. This can be made up to several days in advance. Keep in the fridge.

BACON BREAD SPIRALS

Fun to make, even more fun to eat.

SERVES 4
400G (14OZ) STRONG FLOUR
150ML (5FL OZ) WATER
1 TSP DRIED YEAST
1 TSP SALT
2 TBSP OLIVE OIL, PLUS EXTRA FOR GREASING
16 RASHERS OF STREAKY BACON

Mix the flour, water, yeast, salt and oil together to form a dough. Put into a lightly oiled bowl, cover with a damp cloth and leave to rise in a warm place for 45 minutes until doubled in size.

Preheat the oven to 180°C/350°F/Gas Mark 4.

Give the dough a quick knead then roll it into two long, thin sausages. Wrap 8 rashers of bacon around each dough sausage and form each into a spiral.

Place on a lightly greased baking tray and bake in the oven for 15–18 minutes until the bacon is nice and golden, keeping a close eye on them to make sure they don't burn.

TARTE FLAMBÉE

A fancy name for bacon pizza.

MAKES 1 LARGE PIZZA
400G (14OZ) STRONG FLOUR, PLUS EXTRA FOR SPRINKLING
150ML (5FL OZ) WATER
1 TSP DRIED YEAST
1 TSP SALT
2 TBSP OLIVE OIL, PLUS EXTRA FOR GREASING
10 RASHERS OF STREAKY BACON (OR 150G/5OZ BACON BITS)
200ML (7FL OZ) CRÈME FRAÎCHE
1 ONION, PEELED AND FINELY CHOPPED

Mix the flour, water, yeast, salt and oil together to form a dough. Put into a lightly oiled bowl, cover with a damp cloth and leave to rise in a warm place for 45 minutes (or for several hours in the fridge). Preheat the oven to 250°C/475°F/Gas Mark 9.

Chop the bacon into smallish pieces, unless you're using bacon bits. Give the dough a quick knead then roll it out on a lightly floured work surface to form a pizza base, then slide it onto a lightly floured baking sheet. Whip the crème fraîche until stiff and spread it on to the base, then sprinkle with the onion and bacon. Bake in the oven for approximately 10 minutes, keeping a close eye on it to make sure it doesn't burn.

Bacon makes babies brainier

YOU'VE GOT A bun in the oven? The smartest thing you can do to make your baby smarter is to fire up the oven! Researchers at the University of North Carolina have discovered that the chemical choline, which is found in bacon, can improve brain development in foetuses, specifically in the regions of the brain that process memory.

If it wasn't good enough that this substance is found in bacon, it's also found in eggs! God must have been having a good day at the office when He came up with that one. You're welcome!

SOURCE: FORSKNING.NO

MACARONI-CHEESE MUFFINS WITH BACON

Bacon is as welcome in a muffin as anywhere else.

MAKES 12 MUFFINS

12 RASHERS OF BACK OR
STREAKY BACON
500G (1LB 2OZ) MACARONI
100G (3½OZ)
BREADCRUMBS
4 TBSP FINELY GRATED
PARMESAN CHEESE

FOR THE WHITE SAUCE

150G (5OZ) BUTTER, PLUS
EXTRA FOR GREASING
2 TBSP PLAIN FLOUR, PLUS
EXTRA FOR DUSTING
250ML (9FL OZ) MILK
400G (14OZ) GRATED
CHEDDAR CHEESE
SALT AND FRESHLY
GROUND BLACK PEPPER

Preheat the oven to 200°C/400°F/Gas Mark 6.

Line a baking tray with baking paper. Lay the bacon slices out on the tray and cook in the oven for approximately 12 minutes. Remove from the oven and, once it has cooled, chop the bacon and set aside.

Grease 12 cups of a muffin tin with a little of the butter or use paper muffin cups. Dust with a little of the flour, tipping off the excess.

Cook the macaroni in a pan of boiling water until al dente, then drain off the water and set aside.

To make the white sauce, melt 3 tablespoons of the butter in a saucepan. Sift in the flour and stir vigorously with a whisk. After 1–2 minutes, slowly pour in the milk, a little at a time, stirring constantly. Let it simmer a little between adding each splash of milk. Stir until the white sauce thickens, then add the cheese and stir into the sauce. Let it melt until the sauce is smooth. Take off the heat and pour in the cooked macaroni and the bacon.

Stir together the remaining butter, the breadcrumbs and the finely grated Parmesan. Fill the muffin cups right to the brim with the macaroni mixture and top each one with a sprinkling of the Parmesan mixture.

Bake in the oven for 15–20 minutes until cooked through and the muffins look nice and browned. Take them out of the oven and leave to cool. You can eat them slightly warm or store them in the fridge once cooled.

«Let's see, Farmer Billy's smoke-fed bacon, Farmer Billy's bacon-fed bacon, Farmer Billy's travel bacon... Mr Simpson, if you really want to kill yourself, I also sell handguns!»
APU NAHASAPEEMAPETILON, *The Simpsons*

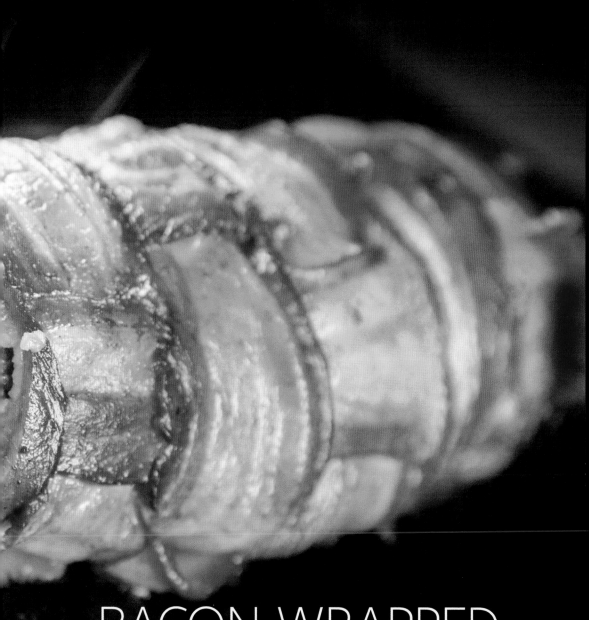

BACON-WRAPPED MEATLOAF

SEE RECIPE, OVERLEAF »

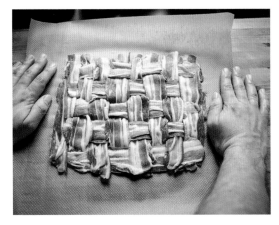

BACON-WRAPPED MEATLOAF

Weaving isn't just for thread.

SERVES 6

½ ONION, PEELED AND CHOPPED
OIL, FOR FRYING
1 GARLIC CLOVE, PEELED AND CRUSHED
3 TBSP CHOPPED FLAT-LEAF PARSLEY
½ GREEN OR RED PEPPER, DESEEDED AND CHOPPED
14 RASHERS OF STREAKY BACON
500G (1LB 2OZ) BEEF MINCE
SALT AND FRESHLY GROUND BLACK PEPPER

Preheat the oven to 180°C/350°F/Gas Mark 4.

Fry the onion in a little oil until golden. Add the garlic, parsley and chopped pepper and fry for another couple of minutes. Set to one side.

Spread a large piece of baking paper over a clean work surface. Weave the bacon: Lay 7 rashers of bacon alongside each other vertically on the paper. On every other strip of bacon, fold over the end enough that you can lay the first horizontal slice underneath them. Fold the slices back over the top. Repeat the process with the second horizontal slice, folding up the other vertical slices, this time to slot in another strip of bacon, so that you are alternating horizontal strips and creating a lattice pattern. Repeat until you have a large woven-lattice sheet.

Mix the mince with a little salt and pepper. Form it into a rectangle on top of the bacon, a little smaller than the sheet of bacon. Spread the fried vegetables in a horizontal strip across the middle of the meat. Lift the baking paper carefully and fold the bacon over and around the meat, pressing it carefully together to form a tight sausage. Remove the baking paper, place the sausage on a baking tray and cook it in the oven for approximately 45 minutes or until the bacon looks crisp and golden. It's advisable to turn it over halfway through, otherwise the bacon underneath won't get crispy.

BACON RISOTTO

Pay attention to the way people close their eyes as they eat bacon risotto.

SERVES 2

10 RASHERS OF BACK OR STREAKY BACON (OR 150G/5oz BACON BITS)
1 ONION, PEELED AND FINELY CHOPPED
OIL, FOR FRYING
1 GARLIC CLOVE, PEELED AND CRUSHED
200G (7oz) RISOTTO RICE (ARBORIO RICE)
100ML (3½FL OZ) WHITE WINE
700ML (1 PINT 3½FL OZ) CHICKEN STOCK
1 HANDFUL DRIED PORCINI MUSHROOMS
75G (3oz) FRESHLY GRATED PARMESAN CHEESE
3 TBSP BUTTER
1 TBSP CHOPPED CHIVES
PARMESAN CHEESE SHAVINGS, TO SERVE

Preheat the oven to 200°C/400°F/Gas Mark 6. Line a baking tray with baking paper. Spread the bacon rashers out on the tray and bake for approximately 12 minutes or until the bacon is nice and golden, or cook the bacon pieces in a dry pan. Remove the bacon from the oven and, once it has cooled, chop into small pieces as necessary.

Fry the onion in a little oil in a large saucepan until golden. Add the garlic and rice to the saucepan and fry for a couple of minutes. Pour in the wine and most of the chicken stock. Crush the porcini mushrooms with your hands, add them to the pan and bring to the boil.

Reduce the heat and simmer the risotto for approximately 17 minutes or until all the liquid has been absorbed by the time the rice is cooked. Add more stock if needed, stirring occasionally. Stir the cheese, butter and bacon into the rice. Serve sprinkled with freshly chopped chives and shaved Parmesan.

BACON MEATBALLS WITH RAISINS AND PINE NUTS

False modesty aside: these are the world's greatest meatballs.

SERVES 4

10 RASHERS OF BACK OR STREAKY BACON
3 TBSP PINE NUTS
3 SLICES OF BREAD, CRUSTS REMOVED
1 EGG
2 GARLIC CLOVES, PEELED AND CRUSHED
500G (1LB 2OZ) BEEF MINCE
3 TBSP FRESHLY GRATED PARMESAN CHEESE
2 TBSP CHOPPED FLAT-LEAF PARSLEY
3 TBSP RAISINS
OIL AND BUTTER, FOR FRYING
SALT AND FRESHLY GROUND BLACK PEPPER
PASTA AND TOMATO SAUCE, TO SERVE

Preheat the oven to 200°C/400°F/Gas Mark 6. Line an oven tray with baking paper.

Spread out the rashers of bacon on the tray and bake for approximately 12 minutes or until golden. Once it has cooled down, finely chop the bacon.

Put the pine nuts in a dry frying pan over a medium heat and leave until lightly browned – don't let them burn. Put the bread in cold water for 2–3 minutes. Whisk the egg in a large bowl. Add the garlic to the bowl along with the mince, bacon pieces, Parmesan, parsley, pine nuts, raisins, salt and pepper. Squeeze the water out of the bread with your hands and add the bread to the bowl. Mix the ingredients thoroughly, so the bread breaks up evenly.

Form the mixture into meatballs – decide for yourself how big you want them to be. Some prefer to make 12 extra-large meatballs, while others prefer to make 24 (about the size of a classic 'Swedish meatball'). Fry them in butter and oil until they're golden brown with a nice crispy exterior. Best served with pasta and tomato sauce.

PASTA CARBONARA

The Italians know what it's all about!

SERVES 2

10 RASHERS OF BACK OR STREAKY BACON
(OR 150G/5oz BACON BITS)
75G (3oz) PARMESAN CHEESE, FINELY GRATED
5 TBSP DOUBLE CREAM
3 EGGS
250G (9oz) SPAGHETTI
SALT AND FRESHLY GROUND BLACK PEPPER

Fry the bacon in a dry pan until crispy. Once it has cooled down, chop the bacon into small pieces and put them in a heatproof bowl, along with the Parmesan and cream. Break the eggs into the bowl and lightly whisk them, adding salt and pepper to taste.

Cook the pasta according to your preference, in well-salted boiling water. Drain, then pour the warm pasta immediately into the bowl with the bacon and other ingredients. Stir well and serve immediately.

Probably the best bacon order ever made

THE LEGENDARY Tor Milde (RIP), Norwegian music journalist and writer was responsible for the world's only documented 'quadruple side order of bacon'.

The order was placed in New York in autumn 1998 and was part of a breakfast comprising an enormous blue cheese omelette, pommes frites, a rack of bread and an extra-large portion of beans. Reliable witnesses confirm that Milde ate his plate completely clean and left the restaurant under his own steam.

PHOTO: PRIVATE

BURNING LOVE

This must be what Elvis was singing about.

SERVES 2, AS A SIDE
5 RASHERS OF BACK OR STREAKY BACON
 (OR 90G/SCANT 3½oz BACON BITS)
½ RED ONION, CHOPPED
OIL, FOR FRYING
5 POTATOES, PEELED AND CHOPPED
3 TBSP BUTTER
2 TBSP CHOPPED CHIVES

Fry the bacon until crispy (either in a frying pan or for approximately 12 minutes on baking paper on a baking tray in a 200°C/400°F/Gas Mark 6 oven). Once it has cooled down, chop the bacon into small pieces.

Fry the red onion in a little oil until soft. Boil the potatoes until they're soft, then drain and mash them with the butter.

Serve the mashed potato with the onion, chopped bacon and chives. Decide for yourself if you want to mix them together before serving or not.

 ## Elvis' Fool's Gold Loaf

ONE OF ELVIS' favourite foods was Fool's Gold Loaf: a whole loaf of white bread, warmed then sliced in two, hollowed out, filled with a jar of jam, a jar of peanut butter and half a kilo of crispy fried bacon. This marvel contained an artery-clogging 8,000 calories. Elvis once snuck into the Colorado Gold Mine Company restaurant in Denver, where the sandwich originated, disguised as a police officer to taste it.

According to Nick Andurlakis,

the chef behind the sandwich, the story goes that Elvis had visitors at home at Graceland, and they started talking about this culinary wonder. They fired each other up so much that in the end they bundled into Elvis' private jet and flew 2 hours to Denver. By the time they arrived at the airport, in the middle of the night, 22 loaves were waiting for them in a special hangar. They spent three gluttonous hours there, washing the sandwiches down

with champagne, then they flew back home.

The Colorado Gold Mine Company doesn't exist any more, but Nick still serves the sandwich at his café – 'Nick's Café' – in Golden, Colorado.

Another legendary sandwich to bear Elvis' name contains peanut butter, banana and bacon – ideally, fried in bacon fat.

The King clearly took his bacon seriously!

SOURCES: WIKIPEDIA.COM,
DENVERPOST.COM

PASTA SAUCE WITH BEER AND BACON

It was about time bacon and beer were combined in one pasta sauce.

SERVES 4
2 SHALLOTS, PEELED AND CHOPPED
1 GARLIC CLOVE, PEELED AND CRUSHED
1 TSP DRIED THYME
5 RASHERS OF BACK OR STREAKY BACON, CHOPPED
 (OR 75G/3OZ BACON BITS)
2 TBSP CHOPPED RED PEPPER
2 TBSP BUTTER
2 TBSP PLAIN FLOUR
100ML (3½FL OZ) LIGHT BEER
100ml (3½FL OZ) MILK, PLUS EXTRA TO THIN
½ TSP CAYENNE PEPPER
½ TSP SMOKED PAPRIKA POWDER
200G (7OZ) GRATED CHEESE
SALT AND FRESHLY GROUND BLACK PEPPER
PASTA, TO SERVE

Fry the shallots, garlic, thyme, bacon and red pepper in the butter until the onion is golden. Sprinkle the flour over the top and fry for a few minutes, stirring constantly.

Pour in the beer and bring to the boil as you stir. Add the milk and continue to let it boil, stirring. Add more milk if the sauce becomes too thick.

Season to taste with the cayenne pepper, smoked paprika, salt and pepper, then simmer for 8–10 minutes. Add the cheese and let it melt. Serve the sauce with pasta of your choice.

Quantity training

IN NEW YORK in 2013 more than 100 volunteers turned up for an attempt to beat the world record for the number of sandwiches made in one hour. The participants used almost 550kg (1,212lb) of bacon, 6,000 slices of cheese and 76kg (167½lb) of lettuce, putting together 2,706 sandwiches and breaking the previous measly record of 1,660 by a wide margin. The stunt was to raise money and awareness for veterans and their families.

SOURCE: WORLDRECORDACADEMY.COM

BACON QUESADILLAS

These are just standing here, waiting for you to get bored of tacos.

MAKES 4

1 ONION, PEELED AND FINELY CHOPPED
15 RASHERS OF BACK OR STREAKY BACON (PREFERABLY ENGLISH
   BACK BACON), CUT INTO SMALL PIECES
OIL, FOR FRYING
2 TBSP TACO SPICE MIX
200G (7OZ) BEEF MINCE
1 DICED RED CHILLI
2 SPRING ONIONS, TRIMMED AND DICED
4 TBSP CREAM CHEESE
4 TORTILLAS
1 TSP GROUND CORIANDER
GRATED CHEDDAR CHEESE, FOR SPRINKLING

Preheat the oven to its lowest setting.

Fry the onion and bacon in a little oil until golden. Add the taco spice mix and the mince, then stir and add the chilli and spring onions, breaking up the mince with a wooden spoon. Fry until browned.

Spread the cream cheese over the tortillas and dress with a sprinkling of coriander. Spread the mince and bacon mixture over half of each tortilla, then fold the other half over the top.

Fry the tortillas in a clean frying pan until golden, then flip them over and fry the other sides. To finish, sprinkle a little cheese over the top and place the tortillas in the oven to melt the cheese.

«I'd eat my own foot if it was wrapped in bacon
and cooked in butter.»

DOUG HEFFERNAN, *The King of Queens*

«When you have bacon in your mouth,
it doesn't matter who's president or anything…
Every time I'm eating bacon I think,
I could die right now, and I mean it.
That's how good life is.»
COMEDIAN LOUIS CK

NACHOS WITH CHEESE AND BACON SAUCE

They sound great, they look great, and they taste amazing.

SERVES 4
10 RASHERS OF BACK OR STREAKY BACON (OR 150G/5oz BACON BITS)
2 TBSP BUTTER
2 TBSP PLAIN FLOUR
200ML (7FL OZ) MILK
1 PINCH OF SALT
1 PINCH OF CAYENNE PEPPER
150G (5oz) GRATED CHEDDAR CHEESE
NACHOS, TO SERVE

Preheat the oven to 200°C/400°F/Gas Mark 6. Line a baking tray with baking paper. Lay the bacon slices out on the tray and bake for approximately 12 minutes. If you aren't using pre-chopped bacon bits cooked in a dry pan, once it has cooled down chop the bacon into pieces.

Melt the butter in a saucepan. Pour in the flour and stir constantly for 1–2 minutes. Add the milk, a little at a time, whisking steadily. Bring the sauce back to the boil every time you add milk.

When it is thick and smooth, season to taste with the salt and cayenne pepper. Add the cheese and let it melt – the sauce will be completely smooth if you just leave the cheese to melt slowly and steadily. Stir in the bacon pieces.

Serve the sauce over nachos. (If you want, you can heat the nachos in the oven at 110°C/225°F/Gas Mark ¼ before pouring the sauce over them.)

BACON ONION RINGS

The world's greatest onion rings.

MAKES 4
1 ONION, PEELED
12 RASHERS OF STREAKY BACON
DIPPING SAUCE OF YOUR CHOICE, TO SERVE

Preheat the oven to 180°C/350°F/Gas Mark 4. Line a baking tray with baking paper.
Cut the onion into four large rings from the thickest part of the onion. You can save the
rest of the onion for something else.

Wrap three rashers of bacon around each onion ring and place on the baking tray.

Bake in the oven for approximately 20 minutes or until the bacon is golden and crispy.
Pay attention to make sure they don't burn.

You can spice the rings up a little by dipping them in BBQ sauce, or a homemade
version using 2 tablespoons of ketchup, 1 teaspoon of brown sugar and a little soy sauce.

'The Bacon Show'

THE BLOG 'The Bacon Show' was started by a man who thought it was entirely possible to post a bacon recipe per day, every day, for ever. So far, he's kept it up since 2005 – and it doesn't look like he'll be stopping any time soon.

On the blog you can find anything from traditional recipes for BLTs and bacon burgers, to some rather more exotic variants, such as bacon with kangaroo sausages and alligator tail.

SOURCE: BACONSHOW.BLOGSPOT.COM

«Yes, I'll have a non-fat, decaf latte, please. Oh, what the hell! Look,
make it a full-fat mocha with extra whipped cream.
What the hell, put a slice of bacon on it!»

DR FRASIER CRANE, *Frasier*

DEVILS ON HORSEBACK

A classic that is often served as a canapé.

MAKES 4

2 RASHERS OF BACK OR
  STREAKY BACON
4 PITTED DATES
1 SPRIG OF THYME
CHILLI SAUCE, TO SERVE

Cut each rasher in two then wrap each piece around a date and sprinkle with thyme leaves. Fry in a dry frying pan until the bacon is golden on both sides. Serve with chilli sauce.

You can also cook them in the oven. Set the oven to 200°C/400 Gas Mark 6. Place the bacon-wrapped dates on a baking tray lined with baking paper and cook for 1 minutes, then check. Do they look done, or could they use another couple of minutes?

TIP!

• Some people like to stuff the d with cheese, mango chutney, o other goodies.

DEEP-FRIED BACON BITES

A mouthful of delight – in only 90 seconds.

MAKES 6
50G (2OZ) CHÈVRE (GOAT'S CHEESE)
100G (3½OZ) BEEF MINCE
6 RASHERS OF BACK OR STREAKY BACON
SUNFLOWER OIL, FOR DEEP-FRYING

Split the cheese and roll into 6 small balls, about the size of marbles. Wrap some of the mince around each ball, as thinly as you can manage. Wrap a rasher of bacon around the mince – it's easier than you think!

Heat enough oil to deep-fry the balls in a deep pan to approximately 170°C – use a cooking thermometer and pay close attention. Fry the balls for approximately 90 seconds, then remove with a slotted spoon and drain on a rack lined with kitchen paper.

The bites can be eaten hot, but they are just as good at room temperature.

Bacon festival

FOR THE ABOVE averagely bacon-obsessed, it might be worth keeping an eye on Blue Ribbon. What began as a group of Iowa boys' unpretentious homage to bacon grew rapidly, culminating in a dedicated Bacon Festival in 2008, which has been arranged annually ever since. If your timing is good, you can even attend their Bacon University, where you'll receive a comprehensive education in ... bacon.

Over time it's also developed to include a sort of bacon tour, allowing other regions, even other countries, to experience the joys of organised bacon celebrations.

In the summer of 2015 they took a trip all the way to Reykjavik, in Iceland. They also arrange a 30km (18½ mile) BACooN bike ride – about as far as you can get from the Tour de France – back home in Iowa.

Worth keeping an eye on – before you know it, there'll be a bacon festival near you!

SOURCE:
BLUERIBBONBACONFESTIVAL.COM

BACON BALLS IN PASTRY

'If these taste as good as they look, this is how I want to die.'

MAN, 43

MAKES 4 BALLS
4 CUBES OF CHEDDAR CHEESE
100G (3½OZ) BEEF MINCE
2 RASHERS OF BACK OR STREAKY BACON, CUT IN HALF
1 SHEET OF PUFF PASTRY
SUNFLOWER OIL, FOR DEEP-FRYING

Wrap each cube of cheese in mince. Wrap bacon around each ball – half a slice should be enough. Divide the pastry into 4 pieces and wrap a piece around each ball.

Heat enough oil to deep-fry the balls in a deep pan to approximately 170ºC – use a cooking thermometer and pay close attention. Fry the balls for approximately 90 seconds or until crisp and golden, then remove with a slotted spoon and drain on kitchen paper.

Bacon-MC

THE QUEST FOR alternative, environmentally friendly fuels has turned up some strange things. Among the stranger ones: bacon fat.

The American food company Hormel has rebuilt a diesel motorbike, apparently one of only 20 of its type in the world, so it can run on 100 per cent refined bacon fat. The fat has been converted to 100 per cent biodiesel, which as well as being carbon neutral has reduced levels of other emissions. Another plus is that the exhaust fumes smell of bacon!

The bike runs about as well on bacon fat as it does on diesel, and it doesn't cost much more to turn bacon into fuel than it does to produce fuel in a more conventional way. The raw materials do, however, set some limitations.

You need almost 3.5kg (7¾lb) of bacon to make just under 1 litre (1¾ pints) of fat and you need more than 1 litre (1¾ pints) of fat to produce 1 litre (1¾ pints) of fuel.

But, on the plus side, now there's something else you can do with the leftover fat from breakfast! And then you can drive to the shops to buy more bacon, to make more biodiesel, to drive to the shops to buy ... you get the picture.

SOURCES: BACONBIKE.COM, CNBC.COM

«Now I know what a piece of bacon feels like when it is suddenly picked
out of the pan on a fork and put back on the shelf!»
«No you don't!» he heard Dori answering, «because the bacon knows
that it will get back in the pan sooner or later; and it is to be hoped we
shan't. Also eagles aren't forks!»

J.R.R. TOLKIEN, *The Hobbit*

FAMOUS BACONS

SIR FRANCIS BACON, 'the father of empiricism', English author, philosopher, jurist and pioneer of the scientific method, who lived at the turn of the 1500s and 1600s. He died as a result of his own scientific experiments: he developed a lung infection while investigating how freezing worked as a preservation method for – ironically enough – meat.

FRANCIS BACON, a painter, who mustn't be confused with his namesake (although they are believed to be distantly related). Irish-born figurative painter, best known for his raw, sometimes brutal imagery. He died in 1992, and the price of his paintings has skyrocketed ever since.

CLARA SALTER BACON, renowned mathematician who in 1911 became the first woman in the USA to receive a PhD in mathematics from the prestigious Johns Hopkins University.

DELIA SALTER BACON, American author from the 1900s, known for her plays and short stories. She was a good friend of the authors Nathaniel Hawthorne and Ralph Waldo Emerson and in 1832 she won a short-story prize right under the nose of Edgar Allan Poe.

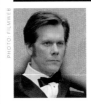

KEVIN BACON, actor who charmed the world with his incredible dance moves in the 1980s movie *Footloose* (he later admitted that he didn't perform them himself), still going strong after almost 40 years in the business. He is also the centre of the game 'Six Degrees of Kevin Bacon', where the goal is to link a celebrity to Kevin Bacon in six links or less, the fewer connections the better. The game was invented by three college students who were snowed in during a snowstorm and began to wonder just how many films Bacon had appeared in and how many different actors he must have worked with. The game has since gone on a victory tour on various talk shows, including *The Jon Stewart Show*, where Bacon himself joined in.

SOURCES: REPUBLICOFBACON.COM, WIKIPEDIA.COM

BACON
BOMBS

SEE RECIPE,
OVERLEAF »

BACON BOMBS

Probably best if the Department of Health doesn't find out about these.

MAKES 1

1 TBSP BBQ SAUCE
2 TBSP BEEF MINCE
1 PIECE OF MOZZARELLA
1 RASHER OF BACK OR STREAKY BACON

Mix the BBQ sauce into the mince. Pack it around the mozzarella and wrap it in the bacon. Secure with cocktail sticks and fry in a dry pan or on a barbecue until the bacon is golden.

J&D's Foods

WHAT WOULD YOU do if you won $5,000 for submitting a home video that was shown on *America's Funniest Home Videos*?

Start a business, of course. A bacon business.

J&D's Foods is a company from Seattle, with the motto 'Everything should taste like bacon', founded by friends Justin and Dave, using Dave's prize money. The company produces an astonishing range of bacon products and sold 6,000 tins of its Bacon Salt in just five days – without spending anything on marketing. Since then, they've come out with everything from bacon mayonnaise to bacon popcorn to bacon soda – none of the ingredients include actual bacon ...

One of their stranger products is their bacon lube, which was an April Fool's joke that went 'wrong' when people went completely bananas for it.

The natural next step was, of course, making a bacon condom – a completely normal condom, that both smells and tastes like bacon.

Their other bacon products include shaving cream, envelopes (which taste of bacon when you lick the glue on the flap), lip balm, deodorant and sun cream. They've even made bacon coffins! For real funerals. For people who, it seems, wish to rest in eternity with bacon.

They've also achieved several records, such as the first bacon salt to ascend Kilimanjaro and to trick *TIME* magazine into writing an article about the production of the mysterious product 'BaconAir', a bacon-flavoured oxygen inhaler made from 95 per cent pure oxygen from the Himalayas. Really.

SOURCES: JDFOODS.NET, HUFFINGTONPOST.COM

POTATO SKINS WITH SOURED CREAM AND BACON

Perfect snacks for someone with a bit of a craving.

MAKES 4

2 LARGE POTATOES
OIL, FOR GREASING
10 RASHERS OF BACK OR STREAKY BACON
4 TBSP SOURED CREAM
1 TBSP CHOPPED FRESH TARRAGON

Preheat the oven to 200°C/400°F/Gas Mark 6. Cut the potatoes in two. Add a little oil to a heatproof baking tray and lay the potatoes on it, cut-side down, then bake for 50–60 minutes.

Fry the bacon until crispy (either in a frying pan or for approximately 12 minutes on baking paper on a baking tray alongside the potatoes in the oven). Once it has cooled down, chop the bacon into small pieces and stir most of it into the soured cream, then add tarragon to taste.

When the potatoes are done, use a teaspoon to scoop out most of the potato flesh and add to the bacon and herby soured cream, then mash it all together. Stuff the mixture back into the potato skins and serve with the remaining bacon bits.

POTATO CAKE WITH BACON

This is for all those days when you can't think of anything else.

SERVES 4, AS A SIDE
10 RASHERS OF BACK OR STREAKY BACON (OR 150G/5OZ BACON BITS)
1KG (2LB 2OZ) POTATOES, PEELED
100G (3½OZ) GRATED CHEDDAR CHEESE
SALT AND PEPPER

Fry the bacon in a dry frying pan until golden, but don't let it get too crispy. Take it out of the pan and set aside.

Cut the potatoes into thin slices. Add them to the pan in which you fried the bacon, cover the pan and fry them on a low heat, turning occasionally, for about 25 minutes. It's good if some of them are very well done and it's no problem if some of them break up a bit.

Meanwhile, if you aren't using pre-chopped bacon bits, chop the bacon into small pieces. Once the potatoes are cooked, add the bacon to the pan, along with the cheese and some salt and pepper to season, and stir well.

Press the mixture together to form a cake – you could use a plate to help shape it. Turn the heat up and let the cake cook for 3–5 minutes – the underside should be well-fried. Squash the cake down occasionally, if necessary. When you see the edges beginning to turn brown, it's ready.

Carefully loosen the edges of the cake and use a spatula to loosen the bottom. You can either lift it out on to a plate, or place a plate on top of it in the pan and flip it upside-down, but take care – the fat in the pan will be hot.

«If you record the sound of bacon in a frying pan and play it back it sounds like the pops and cracks on a old 33 1/3 recording. Almost exactly like that. You could substitute it for that sound.»

TOM WAITS, singer-songwriter

BACON-STUFFED MUSHROOMS

All it lacks is a nice glass of Spanish red wine to drink with it.

MAKES 8
8 CHESTNUT MUSHROOMS
1 ONION, PEELED AND CHOPPED
30G (1¼ OZ) BUTTER
8 RASHERS OF BACK OR STREAKY BACON (OR 120G/4¼ OZ BACON PIECES)
1 SPRIG OF ROSEMARY, CHOPPED
150G (5OZ) GRATED CHEESE

Preheat the oven to 180°C/350°F/Gas Mark 4.

Remove the stalks from the mushrooms, then chop the stalks and set aside. Fry the onion in the butter until golden. Add the chopped mushroom stalks and fry for 5–6 minutes.

Fry the bacon until crispy, either in a frying pan or on baking paper on a baking tray in the oven at 200°C/400°F/Gas Mark 6 for approximately 12 minutes. Once it has cooled down, chop the bacon into small pieces (if you aren't using pre-sliced bacon pieces) and add to the pan with the onion and mushrooms. Remove from the heat, then add the rosemary and cheese to the pan.

Stuff the mushroom tops with the mixture, place on a baking tray and bake them in the oven for 17–20 minutes. Serve immediately.

Bacon in Literature

HENRY IV Part One and The Merry Wives of Windsor are the only Shakespeare plays to mention bacon. Clearly there had to be some downsides to him as well.

«It is the custom on the stage in all good, murderous melodramas, to present the tragic and the comic scenes in as regular alternation as the layers of red and white in a side of streaky, well-cured bacon.»

Charles Dickens

William Shakespeare

BACON AND BRIE QUICHE

Quiche with Brie is good, but quiche with Brie and bacon is even better. Obviously.

SERVES 4, AS A SIDE
15 RASHERS OF BACK OR STREAKY BACON (PREFERABLY THICK CUT)
300G (11OZ) PLAIN FLOUR
150G (5OZ) BUTTER
3 TBSP COLD WATER
150G (5OZ) BRIE
3 EGGS
300ML (11FL OZ) MILK
2 SPRING ONIONS, TRIMMED AND CUT INTO SMALL PIECES
3 TBSP FINELY CHOPPED FRESH THYME
1 TSP SALT
FRESHLY GROUND BLACK PEPPER

Preheat the oven to 200°C/400°F/Gas Mark 6. Line a baking tray with baking paper. Lay the bacon slices out on the tray and cook for approximately 12 minutes. Once it has cooled down, chop the bacon into pieces.

Increase the oven temperature to 220°C/425°F/Gas Mark 7.

Mix the flour and butter in a food processor until they resemble breadcrumbs. Gradually add 1 tablespoon of cold water at a time, mixing together into a smooth pastry dough.

Line a pie dish with the dough and prick holes in it using a fork. Bake in the oven for 10 minutes, then remove.

Reduce the oven temperature to 200°C/400°F/Gas Mark 6.

Cut the Brie into large pieces and spread them across the pie dish. Distribute the bacon over the whole base. Whisk the eggs and milk in a bowl. Stir in the spring onions along with the thyme and season with the salt and some black pepper to taste. Pour the mixture over the bacon and bake in the oven for 35–40 minutes until the pastry is golden and the filling has set.

CAULIFLOWER GRATIN WITH BACON

I was practically raised on this gratin. I wouldn't have had it any other way.

SERVES 4, AS A SIDE
10 RASHERS OF BACK OR STREAKY BACON (PREFERABLY THICK-CUT)
1 HEAD OF CAULIFLOWER, CHOPPED INTO SMALL FLORETS
3 EGGS
200ML (7FL OZ) MILK
200G (7OZ) GRATED CHEESE
FRESHLY GRATED NUTMEG
SALT AND FRESHLY GROUND BLACK PEPPER

Preheat the oven to 200°C/400°F/Gas Mark 6.

Line a baking tray with baking paper. Lay the bacon slices out on the tray and bake for approximately 10 minutes. It shouldn't get too crispy.

Cook the cauliflower florets in boiling water for 3 minutes, then drain off the water. Put the cauliflower in a heatproof dish.

Whisk together the eggs, milk and grated cheese. Chop up the bacon into large chunks and stir it in, then season with nutmeg, salt and pepper to taste. Pour the mixture over the cauliflower and put it in the oven for approximately 25 minutes or until the cheese is melted and bubbling.

CAULIFLOWER PANCAKES WITH BACON

A new way of making cool, tasty pancakes.

MAKES 6 PANCAKES
1 SMALL HEAD OF CAULIFLOWER, ROUGHLY CHOPPED
2 EGGS
3 TBSP CHOPPED FRESH CORIANDER
6 RASHERS OF BACK OR STREAKY BACON
OIL OR BUTTER, FOR FRYING
SALT AND PEPPER
MAPLE SYRUP OR RUNNY HONEY, TO SERVE

Whizz the cauliflower in a food processor, until the pieces are about the size of small seeds of grain. Tip into a dry frying pan and fry on a low heat for 10–12 minutes, stirring constantly, until most of the liquid has evaporated.

Preheat the oven to 180°C/350°F/Gas Mark 4. Line a baking tray with baking paper.

Whisk together the eggs, cauliflower, coriander, salt and pepper. Divide the cauliflower mixture into six on the baking tray and pat each into a pancake shape, then lay a bacon rasher on top of each circle.

Bake the pancakes for approximately 10 minutes, then turn them over and bake for another 5–6 minutes.

Remove from the oven and, just before serving, fry them in a little oil or butter a frying pan on both sides. They're especially good served with maple syrup or runny honey.

BACON PANCAKES
SEE RECIPE, OVERLEAF »

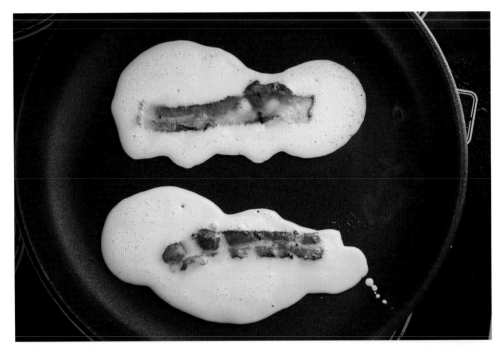

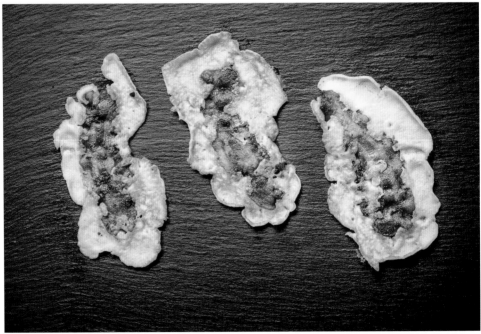

BACON PANCAKES

A breakfast favourite for children, large and small.

MAKES 6
2 EGGS
2 TBSP MELTED BUTTER
250ML (9FL OZ) MILK
200G (8OZ) PLAIN FLOUR
6 RASHERS OF BACK OR STREAKY BACON
SALT

Whisk the eggs in a bowl, then add the melted butter, milk, flour and a pinch of salt. Mix well, then leave to stand for 15 minutes.

Fry the bacon in a dry pan until crispy, then lift out 3 slices and put them on a plate. Leave plenty of room between each of the rashers left in the pan.

Pour a little of the pancake batter over each rasher in the pan and fry them like normal pancakes – until they're golden brown on both sides. Transfer to a plate and repeat with the remaining bacon and batter.

TIP!
• It's easier if you use a bottle to pour in the batter (for example, an empty ketchup or mustard bottle).

BACON POPCORN

Of all the strange things people put on their popcorn, bacon is the best. Obviously.

SERVES 4

6 RASHERS OF BACK OR STREAKY BACON
300G (11OZ) POPCORN
3 TBSP FINELY GRATED PARMESAN CHEESE

Fry the bacon until crispy, either in a frying pan or on baking paper on a baking tray in the oven at 200°C/400°F/Gas Mark 6 for approximately 12 minutes. Reserve the liquid bacon fat.

Once it has cooled down, finely chop the bacon.

Add 2 tablespoons of the bacon fat to a large saucepan. Tip in the popcorn, set on a medium heat and cover the pan. Shake it occasionally, so the corn doesn't burn on the bottom of the pan.

When it's all popped, stir the popcorn thoroughly, so the bacon fat is spread evenly throughout. Stir in the finely grated Parmesan and chopped bacon.

THE ULTIMATE BACON SIDE DISH

The secret weapon that makes everything taste better.

SERVES 2, AS A SIDE
10 RASHERS OF BACK OR STREAKY BACON
25 GREEN BEANS, TRIMMED
2 PEACHES OR NECTARINES, STONED AND CUT INTO CUBES
5 PLUM TOMATOES, CUT INTO HALVES OR QUARTERS
100G (3½OZ) FLAKED ALMONDS
1 TBSP OIL
SQUEEZE OF LEMON JUICE, TO TASTE
SALT AND FRESHLY GROUND BLACK PEPPER

Preheat the oven to 200ºC/400ºF/Gas Mark 6.

Line a baking tray with baking paper. Spread the bacon rashers out on the tray and bake for approximately 12 minutes or until the bacon is nice and golden. Remove the bacon from the oven and, once it has cooled down, chop into small pieces and put in a bowl.

Boil the beans for 2 minutes. Drain off the water, then tip them into the bacon bowl. Add the peaches or nectarines and the tomatoes to the bowl, along with the almonds and oil. Mix well and season with lemon juice, salt and pepper to taste.

Record devouring

AMERICANS ARE PARTICULARLY fond of bacon, eating more than 2.6 *billion* kg (57 billion lb) of it a year. It's not so odd, then, that the man who holds the record for most bacon eaten in 5 minutes is American.

The 55kg (121lb) Matt 'Megatoad'(!) Stonie, at the time ranked at #2 in the international organisation for eating contests, Major League Eating (no, really!

It exists!), smashed the record by more than 120 slices when as a 19 year old in 2015 he hoovered up 182 slices, weighing approximately 2.7kg (6lb), in 5 minutes.

On his already impressive CV, he had also eaten a 6.5kg (14 1/3lb) birthday cake in 8 minutes.

Canadians don't care for always having to play little brother, so their own Peter Czerwinski holds the world

record for drinking a bacon milkshake the fastest, in 1 minute 47.72 seconds. The shake in question filled an entire blender and contained more than 2kg (4lb 4oz) of bacon!

The story doesn't mention if he managed to keep it all down ...

SOURCES: HUFFINGTONPOST.COM, MAJORLEAGUEEATING.COM, RECORDSETTER.COM, REPUBLICOFBACON.COM

BACON
MARSHMALLOWS

SEE RECIPE, OVERLEAF »

BACON MARSHMALLOWS

I always thought that marshmallows were lacking something.

MAKES 1
1 RASHER OF STREAKY BACON
1 MARSHMALLOW

Cook the bacon on a barbecue or fry in a dry pan. When it's cooled enough to handle, roll it around the marshmallow and stick a thin skewer through the bacon and marshmallow. Hold it over the barbecue (or campfire) until the marshmallow melts.

Eat it just the way you would a normal marshmallow – straight from the skewer!

God's – and the Foo Fighters' – currency

THE ROCK BAND Foo Fighters are so obsessed with bacon that they've included it on their tour rider, to make sure they have it available backstage at all their concerts.

'Bacon. I call it God's currency.

Hell, if it could be breathed, I would. Bacon in any form is great. Not as an entrée, but just in general.'

In a later rider, they added that 'French pastries are not an acceptable substitute for a real breakfast prominently featuring bacon.' And just in case you still haven't grasped the seriousness of all this: 'Seriously, don't forget the damned bacon.'

SOURCE: THESMOKINGGUN.COM

BACON CHOCOLATE

The explosion when two of the world's greatest flavours collide in your mouth.

MAKES 8

8 RASHERS OF BACK OR
  STREAKY BACON
200G (7OZ) COOKING CHOCOLATE
CHOPPED NUTS OR FLAKED
ALMONDS, TO DECORATE
  (OPTIONAL)

Fry the bacon in a dry pan until golden and lay it out on kitchen paper. Press the paper over both sides of the bacon to get rid of the excess fat.

Melt the chocolate carefully, preferably in a heatproof bowl over a pan of boiling water. Do as little as possible until the chocolate has melted.

Dip the rashers of bacon in the chocolate and lay them on baking paper. Cool them in the fridge.

Once set, you can dip them in the chocolate one more time, and cool again, if you want an even thicker chocolate coating.

Decorate with chopped nuts or flaked almonds, if you like.

BACON-AND-EGG ICE CREAM

All of us who've claimed to have discovered this ... we actually stole it from the famous Fat Duck restaurant, outside London.

SERVES 4

6 RASHERS OF STREAKY BACON
200ML (7FL OZ) MILK
200ML (7FL OZ) DOUBLE CREAM
3 EGG YOLKS
150G (5OZ) SUGAR

Fry the bacon in a dry pan as you like it and, when it's cool enough to handle, cut it into small pieces. Combine the milk and cream in a bowl, then tip the bacon pieces into the mix and leave to stand, preferably overnight in the fridge.

Whisk the egg yolks and sugar vigorously, in a heatproof bowl. Pour the milk, cream and bacon mixture into a saucepan and heat to boiling point. Pour it slowly over the whisked eggs, whisking constantly. Pour the mixture into an ice-cream maker, or put it in the freezer. If you use the freezer, you should stir the mixture every half hour or so (until it freezes) to avoid ice crystals forming.

Bacon and egg ice cream

IT WAS CELEBRITY chef Heston Blumenthal who first came up with Bacon and Eggs Ice Cream. It's still served at his three-Michelin star restaurant The Fat Duck, near London. Earlier in his career Blumenthal achieved considerable success with this sort of unconventional dish. 'Snail Porridge', which is exactly what it sounds like, is another example.

The strangest thing is that it's all really good.

«*Life is too short not to order the bacon dessert.*»
GEORGE TAKEI, best known for playing Hikaru Sulu in *Star Trek*, in his autobiography *Oh Myyy!*

BACON CANDY

Sweet, salty and sinfully good.

MAKES 15
15 RASHERS OF STREAKY BACON
5 TBSP NUTS, PREFERABLY PECAN NUTS
1 TSP CRUSHED PINK PEPPERCORNS
100G (3½OZ) BROWN SUGAR

Preheat the oven to 200°C/400°F/Gas Mark 6. Line a deep-sided baking tray with baking paper. Spread the bacon rashers out on the tray, leaving a little room between each of them.

Grind the nuts, peppercorns and sugar in a food processor until it forms a coarse powder. Pour the powder over the bacon – try to cover each slice completely.

Bake in the oven for 20–30 minutes until the sugar has melted and the bacon is crispy. Leave to cool down, then serve with pride.

Sweet bacon

BACON AND MAPLE syrup is a very popular combination, especially in the USA. Bacon with honey or brown sugar are also common variations. Glazed bacon is the ultimate confectionery for many bacon lovers. Caramel is also a good pairing – the dark, sweet flavour works well with the saltiness and smokiness of bacon.

If you trawl the net, you can find some unbelievable combinations. What do you think about whisky, caramel, bacon and marshmallows? Or bacon, caramel and popcorn? How about bacon, caramel and apples?

You'd struggle to come up with anything that some bacon-obsessed imagination or other hasn't already tried before you.

BACON BISCUITS

You won't find a better beer snack.

MAKES APPROXIMATELY 20
20 RASHERS OF BACK OR STREAKY BACON
250G (9OZ) PLAIN FLOUR, PLUS EXTRA FOR DUSTING
1 TSP SEA SALT
1½ TSP BAKING POWDER
1 TBSP SUGAR
80G (3¼OZ) MELTED BUTTER
80ML (3¼FL OZ) DRY WHITE WINE

Preheat the oven to 200°C/400°F/Gas Mark 6. Line a baking tray with baking paper. Lay the bacon out on the tray and bake until crispy, approximately 12 minutes. Once it has cooled down, finely chop the bacon.

Reduce the oven temperature to 180°C/350°F/Gas Mark 4. Line a baking tray with baking paper.

Thoroughly mix the flour, salt, baking powder and sugar in a bowl. Make a hole in the middle of the flour and pour in the butter and wine. Mix the wet and dry ingredients together using a fork, then press the dough into a ball.

Sprinkle a work surface with flour. Press out the dough and roll with a rolling pin until it's approximately 1.5cm (⅝ in) thick. Cut the dough into small circles, or whatever shape you want your biscuits to be. Spread the biscuits on the baking tray, leaving plenty of room between them, and bake for 15 minutes.

Reduce the oven temperature to 160°C/325°F/Gas Mark 3 and bake for another 15 minutes or until the biscuits are golden. Cool on a wire rack and serve with beer.

Bacon of the month

SOME PLACES IN the world are so bacon-obsessed that they have 'bacon of the month' clubs. These clubs ensure that a new type of bacon is delivered to your door every month, so you always get your fix while also getting to try something new.

SOURCE: BACONFREAK.COM

DRINKS
with bacon

IF YOU ASK a wine expert to recommend a drink that goes well with bacon, you'll get an immediate response:

'Bacon and what?'

'Bacon and eggs, for example?'

'Champagne. It goes with everything.'

For a cauliflower gratin with bacon, your best option is a white Burgundy. If bacon is accompanying another meat, you might be told that red Burgundy is best with chicken, while stronger meat like lamb, beef or game is often best-suited to wines from Rhône, Bordeaux, Piemonte or Toscana.

Some gourmets will always insist that Riesling works with any number of bacon dishes.

But to be honest … beer and bacon is a match made in heaven.

Give me beer and bacon!

Personally, I prefer light beer with bacon. Pilsner is OK, but I prefer blondes, IPAs, amber ales and other light options even more.

Beer enthusiasts can give you more precise instructions, both when it comes to finding the best beer to accompany your food or to find your precise favourite among the multitudinous beers on offer at your local specialist. The possibilities are numerous – some experts will even suggest that sour beers work brilliantly with bacon. I don't actually disagree, but they're definitely an acquired taste.

Myself, I have a guilty pleasure: Lambrusco. Sweet, sparkling wine without so much as a hint of finesse or credibility. It goes brilliantly with bacon.

«But to be honest … beer and bacon is a match made in heaven. Give me beer and bacon!»

BACON BLOODY MARY

Every breakfast needs bacon.

MAKES 2

4 RASHERS OF STREAKY BACON (PREFERABLY THICK CUT)
200ML (7FL OZ) VODKA
400ML (14FL OZ) TOMATO JUICE
WORCESTERSHIRE SAUCE
TABASCO SAUCE (OPTIONAL)
FRESHLY GROUND BLACK PEPPER

It's best if you fry 2 rashers of bacon, dry them on kitchen paper and put them in the vodka the day before.

On the day itself, make sure all the ingredients are cold. Take the bacon slices out of the vodka and eat or discard. Mix the vodka and tomato juice and season with pepper and Worcestershire sauce and a little Tabasco (if using).

Fry the remaining two rashers until crisp and serve one in each glass.

Bacon sandwiches: hangover cure

PHOTO: THINKSOCK.COM

NOT THAT YOU need an excuse to eat a hearty bacon sandwich the morning after the night before, but it's always nice to have a bit of science to back you up.

A survey carried out by researchers at Newcastle University concluded that bacon sandwiches cure hangovers!

The food doesn't absorb the alcohol remaining in the body, as we've been told to believe, but the bread contains plenty of carbohydrates that trigger blood sugar and start it burning, which helps the body to process and get rid of the alcohol faster.

When you drink a lot of alcohol you also slow the chemical reactions in your brain, but the protein-rich bacon contains amino acids that help build these back up, making you feel better.

SOURCES: TELEGRAPH.CO.UK, THETIMES.CO.UK

Make your own
BACON

It's not as hard as you'd think to make your own bacon, but it does take some effort. And equipment.

TO MAKE BACON, pork needs to go through two processes – salting and smoking. Both are simple, but you'll need to put some time into it.

SALTING

SALTING MEAT CAN be done in a number of ways. The first method is dry salting, which is believed to be the original method and also the one that gives the best result.

It's also completely possible to use brine, a more modern technique that was developed for industry. In its simplest form, simply leave the meat in brine for a fixed period – the precise time depends on the thickness of the meat and how salty you want it to be. Industrial salting also involves injections to fill the meat with brine, which is done to make the process go faster. Using brine increases the weight of the meat, and gourmets will be quick to point out that the meat is being – literally – diluted. Bacon made this way is consistently less well regarded – while it can be tempting to go for bacon with a lower price per kilo than bacon without added water (dry salted), know that the difference literally pours away once the water has either evaporated or been left in the pan. So, you need to ask yourself the question – do I want lower-quality bacon, or do I want real bacon made with proper ingredients and no unnecessary additives?

Quality bacon is made by dry salting and that's the technique I'll be using here.

THE MEAT

STREAKY BACON IS primarily made from the belly – the fatty padding on each side of the pig. In America they use a slightly larger portion of the same part of the animal (including some of the ribs). You can ask your butcher (or the meat counter at the supermarket) for a piece of fresh pork belly, which will get you what you're after. If you tell them that you're planning to make bacon, you're unlikely to go wrong.

When you're choosing the meat for your bacon, it's important to know what you want – some people like their bacon fatty, others prefer it lean. Even though standardisation has made pork more reliably similar, there are still differences from pig to pig.

Some like to keep the skin on, but most prefer not to. In principle, you can salt the meat with the skin on and remove it later (either before or after smoking).

For our purposes, we'll be removing the skin before salting. If you leave the skin on for salting, the salt won't be absorbed into the meat as easily and you may need to allow more time for the process.

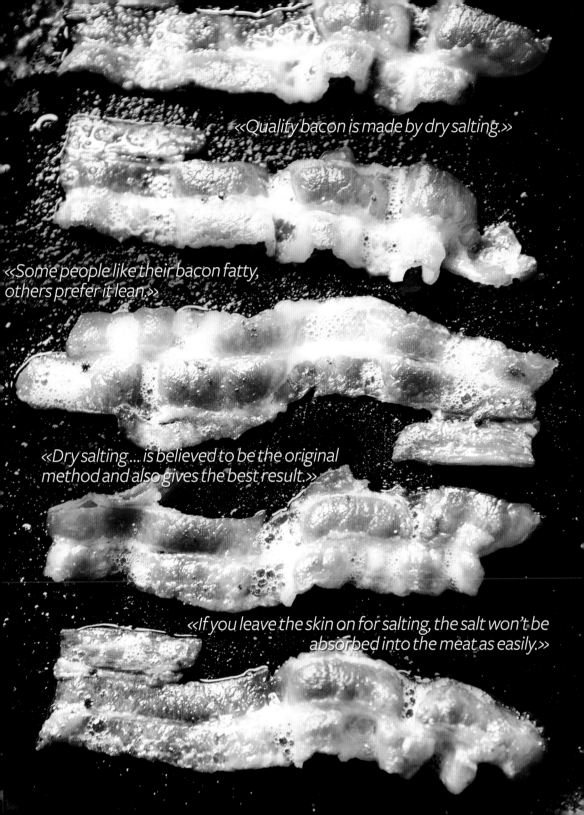

«Quality bacon is made by dry salting.»

«Some people like their bacon fatty,
others prefer it lean.»

«Dry salting .... is believed to be the original
method and also gives the best result.»

«If you leave the skin on for salting, the salt won't be
absorbed into the meat as easily.»

«Using 50 per cent normal salt and 50 per cent nitrite is a typical starting point.»

SALT

There are plenty of things to look out for when you're salting meat. One of the first questions you'll face is whether to use nitrite or not.

Nitrite salt has been used for a long time. The Romans learned about it from the Greeks and its properties have long been known about in India and China.

Nitrite salt is also widely used in the meat industry. In the USA it's required and meat can't legally be described as 'cured' without nitrite salt having been used.

The advantage of nitrite salt is that it gives the meat a fresh, red colour. The nitrites prevent the myoglobin from oxidising, which turns the meat grey. It also hinders the development of botulism. Botulism is rare, but in extreme cases can be deadly (the mortality rate is 5–10 per cent). However, if meat is heated to 85°C (185°F) for longer than 5 minutes or so the bacteria will die anyway.

The reason for controversy surrounding the use of nitrite salt is because there's a possibility that it may be carcinogenic (if it reacts with other chemicals). In most countries nitrites are used in ham, sausages and other cured meats. Nitrite occurs naturally in plants and is even produced by our own bodies.

You should make your own decision, but, for our purposes, we'll be using nitrite. It's not that easy to get hold of – you'll need to order it online. Using 50 per cent normal salt and 50 per cent nitrite is a typical starting point.

In the USA it's common to use some sugar along with the salt, although it's not necessary. It was originally done to prevent the meat from getting too salty, but with modern techniques and knowledge, we no longer need to use as much salt as in the past, so sugar is no longer necessary for that purpose. But there's technically no reason not to use it, either. The sugar results in a slightly sweeter flavour, obviously – it also means that the meat will sometimes get a little bit darker during cooking, as the sugar caramelises. A mix of one-third sugar to two-thirds salt is pretty typical.

Usually the meat will be salted for a week, but some people find that to be too long. You'll soon find out what works best for you.

SEASONING

YOU CAN ALSO use other seasonings. Once you start getting better at making bacon, it's worth testing out some of the other options. If you want to experiment, mix the seasoning with your salt in a food processor before adding it to the meat.

The idea of making your own chilli bacon is certainly tempting. Here are a few options for you to try:

CHILLI
BAY LEAVES (GRIND THEM
 TO A POWDER)
BLACK PEPPER
ROSEMARY AND OTHER WOODY
 HERBS
ROSE PEPPER
CUMIN

DRYING

DRYING MEAT IS traditionally referred to as 'curing'. The process begins after the meat has been salted.

When you make bacon, you start by smoking the meat immediately after the salting is finished, then further curing will take place after smoking. The bacon will develop more flavour if it's left to hang for a while.

It's best to hang meat somewhere well-ventilated – use a pillowcase or mosquito netting around the meat if insects are a problem.

In practice, you'll probably end up using a basement, a storage cupboard or a shed. How long to let the meat hang depends on how successful the salting was, the humidity, the temperature and the condition the meat was in before salting. It's impossible to give an exact suggestion – use your nose, your eyes and your common sense.

HOMEMADE BACON

THERE ARE INNUMERABLE ways to make bacon and once you've gained a bit of experience you'll be able to tailor the recipe according to your own tastes. This is a simple recipe that will give most people everything they need to make their first proper bacon.

PORK BELLY
NITRITE SALT
SUGAR (OPTIONAL)
WOOD CHIPS
A STRONG PLASTIC BAG
 (PREFERABLY ZIPLOCK)
BARBECUE OR SMOKING OVEN
COOKING THERMOMETER
 (PREFERABLY DIGITAL)

For this recipe, we're using 1/3 sugar to 2/3 salt. The precise ratio isn't too important, as long as the meat is completely covered.

SALTING
250G (9OZ) SUGAR
250G (9OZ) NITRITE SALT
250G (9OZ) COARSE SEA SALT
1KG (2LB 2OZ) PORK BELLY,
 WITHOUT SKIN

Combine the sugar and salts in a bowl and roll the meat in the mixture. Put the meat and salt mix into a plastic bag, seal it, place on a plate and put it in the fridge. Leave in the fridge for 1 week, turning the meat and pressing the underside every now and then to make sure the salt covers all of it. A liquid will form around the meat, which is normal.

«There are two main ways to smoke meat: hot smoking and cold smoking.»

THE SMOKE

THERE ARE TWO main ways to smoke meat: hot smoking and cold smoking. The terms are self-explanatory, in that the smoke is hotter during hot smoking. When hot smoking, the meat will also be heat treated.

Bacon is smoked cold. It's a more demanding technique than hot smoking, because you need to maintain tighter control over the temperature which should be 40–60°C (100–140°F).

The easiest way is to try to smoke the bacon in a pellet barbecue. You should put the pellets at one end of the barbecue, with the wood chips on top (ideally, in foil) and the meat at the other end, as far from the pellets as possible. It's not easy to control the temperature of the smoke, so it's not easy to say exactly how long to smoke it. It'll probably work out fine.

If you want more control of the temperature, you'll need more equipment. You can either buy a meat smoker, or build one yourself (see page 181).

The best wood chips to use are juniper, but there's no problem using other types of wood.

People usually stick to deciduous trees (spruce and pine should be avoided, because they contain too much tar), and fruit trees have a particularly fine aroma. It's easy enough to test this for yourself just by burning a dry twig from an apple tree and smelling the distinctive scent of apples.

It's easy to buy online wood chips for smoking. Here are a few options:

JUNIPER	BEECH
OAK	ALDER
HICKORY	CHERRY
APPLE	MAPLE
CHESTNUT	

If you want to try drying the wood yourself, you can do it by heating the dry twigs in an oven at approximately 60°C (140°F) until they're bone dry and can be used for smoking. Break them into chips using an old blender reserved for this purpose.

CARVING

MOST PEOPLE DON'T have access to a machine that can slice bacon as thinly as you'll find it in the shops.

The best way to slice the thinnest bacon without a machine is with a long, sharp knife. The longer the blade of the knife, the easier it is to cut nice smooth, thin slices.

Better and better slicing machines are arriving on the market – they're still expensive and bulky, so only the most dedicated usually stretch that far.

One thing to remember is that cold meat is easier to slice. If you can live with your bacon being half-frozen, it makes the job a lot easier.

SMOKING

YOU'LL NEED 300–400G (11–14oz) of wood chips. Usually the chips you can buy are extremely dry, but if you pour a little bit of water (approximately 25ml/1fl oz water per 100g /3½oz of wood chips) over them a few hours before smoking, you'll get a denser smoke.

Rinse the salt off the meat and dry it very carefully. The surface should be completely dry.

If you're using a smoking oven, the smoke should ideally be set to 40°–60°C (100–140°F). It should not get warmer than this. Put the meat in the oven and leave for 3-4 hours, making sure that there are enough wood chips and that there is plenty of smoke.

If you're using a barbecue, you have to create a hot and a cold zone. With a gas grill, the cold side of the grill should be completely turned off. If you're using a pellet grill, put the pellets at one end and the meat at the other. Take care that the pellets don't get too hot – it's the smoke you're after.

Pack the wood chips in foil, then make a few holes in the package, so the smoke can get out. Put the package over the heat, then place the bacon on the cold side, stick a cooking thermometer into the meat and close the lid. The simplest way is to use a digital cooking thermometer.

Let the meat smoke for about 3 hours. The meat will be done when it hits 65°C (150°F). If the meat doesn't reach this temperature, it's safest to heat it carefully up to 65°C (150°F) in the oven afterwards.

The bacon can be used right away or it can be hung for several days, even weeks. The colder it's stored, the longer it will last.

Build your own
SMOKER

**A SMOKER OVEN CONSISTS
OF THREE PARTS:**
1   HEAT GUN
2   SMOKE GENERATOR
3   SMOKING CHAMBER

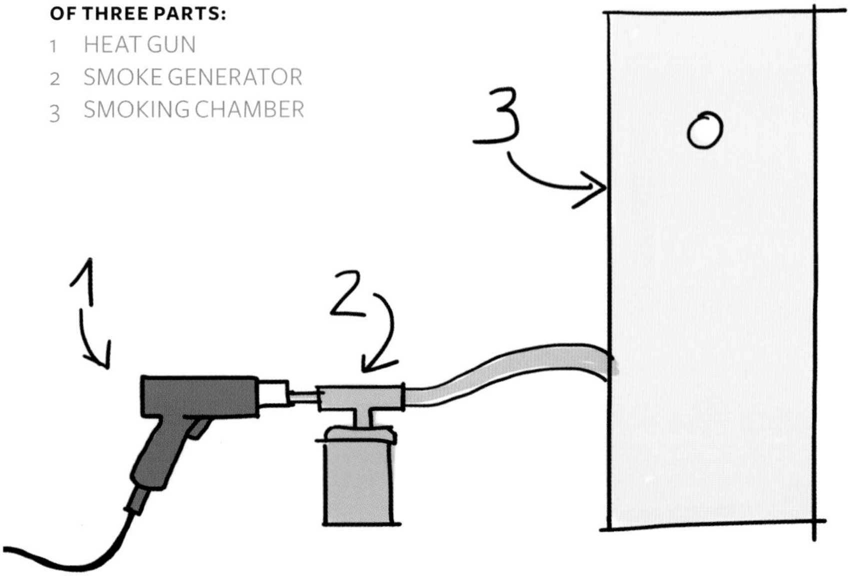

How it works:

The wood chips rest in the smoke generator (2). It's ignited.
The heat gun (1) blows hot air into the box via the pipes, so the wood chips continue to give off smoke. The smoke is blown further into the smoking chamber (3), where the bacon is.

TEMPERATURE

IT'S IMPORTANT TO maintain the correct temperature(40–60°C/100–140°F). You regulate the temperature using the heat gun. The external temperature is also important – in wintry cold it can be harder to get the temperature high enough.

IGNITION AND USE

TIP THE WOOD chips into the box. It's easy enough to light them using a blowtorch. Direct the flame in through the holes, until the chips begin to give out smoke.

Smoking chamber

Smoke generator

Hot air gun

THINGS YOU'LL NEED

HEAT GUN

- You can get one of these for a very reasonable price – make sure you buy one which enable you to set the temperature.
- The best option is to find one with a nozzle that fits the thin copper piping (12mm/ ½in). If it isn't an exact fit, you can use foil to seal it as best you can.

FOR THE SMOKE GENERATOR

- Metal box with a lid (preferably a tea tin)
- Steel plate (you can just use an ordinary food can hammered flat)
- 22mm (⅘in) T-connector (you can buy this from a plumbing store)
- 2 x 22mm (⅘in) pressure nuts
- 2 x 22mm (⅘in) copper pipes, approximately 30cm (12in) long
- 1 x 12mm (½in) copper pipe, approximately 20cm (4¾in) long
- A 22 x 12mm (⅘ x ½in) plumbing nipple Connector between the heat gun and the 12mm (½in) copper pipe

FOR THE SMOKING CHAMBER

- Wooden materials for making the box (eg 15mm x 20mm (⅗ x ¾in) rough timber board and 19mm x 36mm (¾ x 1.4in) purring strips
- The measurements for the box are 35cm x 35cm x 100cm (13¾ x 13¾ x 39⅓in)
- 2 metal air vents (you can buy these at a nautical supplies store)
- Hinges for the door
- 2 metal grills (preferably a thin metal you can cut to size)
- Cooking thermometer (preferably digital)
- Handle for the door

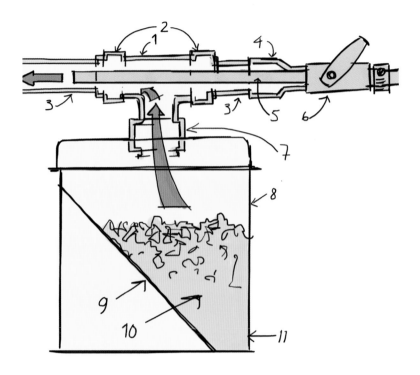

THE SMOKE GENERATOR

THE INPUT IS mainly made of plumbing pipes. If you aren't entirely confident, you can get help from a plumbing store.

In the box (8) are the wood chips. I've fitted a steel plate (9) at an angle, directing the chips down towards the airway.

All the pipes are connected through a clamping system. The T-junction (1) is 22mm and is set down on the top of the lid and fixed in place with a 22mm (⅘in) pressure nut on the bottom. This specific pressure nut (7) isn't entirely standard, so you should check it at the plumbing store.

On each side of the T-junction, fix the two pieces of 22mm (⅘in) copper pipe (3). These should be approximately 70mm (2 ¾in) long. On the other end, fit a 22mm (⅘in) x 12mm (½in) plumbing nipple (4). This can be securely connected (only to the thick pipe), but it isn't necessary to do this.

From the same side, fit the thin pipe that carries the hot air from the heat gun (5). This is 22mm (⅘in) thick and approximately 180mm (7in) long – the most important thing is that the tip goes a little way further in past the point where the smoke comes up. All of this can be a loose piece, that you can just put in place, without fixing it firmly. When you connect the heat gun to the thin pipe, use the largest nozzle – if you don't have one of these you can use foil, wrapped around three times and tightly sealed. Preferably use a hose clamp.

Stick the other end into the smoking chamber.

If you'll be using this for cold smoking, you can replace the heat gun with a compressor or electric air pump. If so, it can be smart to fit a tap (6), so you have complete control of the airflow.

SEE DIRECTIONS FOR SMOKING CHAMBER »

THE SMOKING CHAMBER

THE SMOKING CHAMBER can be anything from a plastic box with a lid to a specially hand-built cabinet. The most important thing is that you should be able to rest or hang the bacon easily and that you can monitor the temperature. If you want to make a wooden cabinet, you can follow these illustrations.

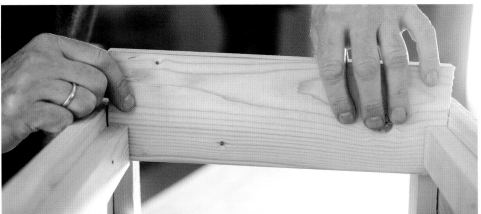

«Is there anywhere in the world a smell as wonderful, as intoxicating, as the smell of fried bacon in the morning?
Is there a smell in the world that can more effectively set a man's heart pounding, his mind racing, his nostrils flaring and his hair to stand on end in delight, gratitude, love, courage, than the smell of fresh coffee in the morning? Ah, breakfast!»

AGNAR MYKLE, AUTHOR

RECIPE INDEX

SOURCES

WHILE WRITING THE history of bacon, I applied the same standards to my own work as I did when working as a research assistant to a history professor. Such strict requirements regarding sources and citations, however, did result in the exclusion of some excellent stories. For example, it is claimed (by numerous people) that a fence had to be erected to keep pigs out of certain parts of Manhattan, and that this fence became known as Wall Street. The journalist in me wants to include this nugget, but the honest historian won out. There are simply too few sources to support the story.

I didn't manage to note all my sources while I was working (as a diligent historian does automatically and without exception), so the following bibliography is far from comprehensive. Much of the history is readily accessible, such as the information on Columbus' voyages, the colonisation of America, and the Industrial Revolution in Britain. Below are some of the most important sources for information on pigs, generally, and bacon in particular. Some of the sources are noted within the text (in which case they are omitted here).

ON THE EARLY HISTORY OF BACON

There are still many aspects of the domestication of pigs that we don't know a great deal about. An interesting article on the BBC's science website tells us that European pigs originated in the Middle East, according to DNA evidence uncovered by researchers. In Europe we then saw a new wave of domestication – of European wild boars. This happened at some point between 7,000 and 4,000 BC.

The Middle Eastern breeds were gradually supplanted and the newer European pigs eventually spread to the Middle East. This is just a hypothesis, but I derived much of the information from this article: http://news.bbc.co.uk/2/hi/science/nature/6978203.stm.

www.touregypt.net/featurestories/pigs.htm gives some information on the early history of pigs in Egypt.

Mark Essig's book *Lesser Beasts: A Snout-to-Tail History of the Humble Pig,* Mark Essig (Basic Books 2015), was an invaluable resource concerning the history of pigs. Many thanks to Mark, who was also very helpful in answering my questions!

www.history.org has several excellent articles on pigs and on the preservation of food by salting and smoking throughout history.

BACON IN ENGLAND

I used many sources to research the early history of bacon – particularly useful was *The Agrarian History of England and Wales: Prehistory* by H.P.R. Finberg, Joan Thirsk (Cambridge U.P.)

The easily accessible public archive at www.railwaysarchive.co.uk was helpful regarding the history of pigs in England and Ireland. On the development of railways in Southern England, the well-documented feasibility studies were useful (they were carried out using more or less random interviews). There are some in Extracts from the *Minutes of Evidence Given Before the Committee of the*

Lords on the London and Birmingham Railway Bill – from 1832, for example.

There is also plenty of worthwhile reading in *Penny Magazine* by the Society for the Diffusion of Useful Knowledge, Volume 12 from 1843.

When it came to information on the Harris family, the article on the subject at www.british-history.ac.uk was a great help.

For those particularly interested, there are actually clips on YouTube, where you can watch the demolition of the fabled bacon factory itself.

I also used *Encyclopaedia of Meat Sciences* by Carrick Devine, and M. Dikeman (Academic Press, 2004).

BACON IN AMERICA

The monumental academic work on the arrival and role of pigs in the New World has, alas, yet to be written. In the meantime, I fell back on a broad and varied array of articles and books. Among them was *The Iberian Pig in Spain and the Americas at the time of Columbus* at www.bzhumdrum.com/pig/iberianpig-intheamericas.pdf.

There are innumerable sites where small pieces of more or less reliable information crop up. A random example is www.austinchronicle.com/food/2009-04-10/764573/, which relates 'the history of the pig in America'. I've fact-checked and attempted to investigate sources for as much of this as I can. The result is the narrative I've assembled in this chapter, and the buck stops with me.

Ann Ramenofsky and Patricia Galloway claim in an article entitled *Sources for the Hernando de Soto Expedition: Intertextuality and the Elusiveness of Truth* that pigs were the cause of the demographic collapse of the indigenous population, particularly by spreading diseases to which the natives lacked immunity (unlike the Europeans). More of this sort of thorough historical analysis would have made the job a lot easier.

THE PIGS OF NEW YORK

Particularly worth reading is *Pigs in New York City; a Study on 19th Century Urban "Sanitation"*, [SIC] by Enrique Alonso and Ana Recarte www.institutofranklin.net/sites/default/files/fckeditor/CS%20Pigs%20in%20New%20York.pdf.

In the section on modern bacon, the excellent *Putting Meat on the American Table: Taste, Technology, Transformation* by Roger Horowitz (The Johns Hopkins University Press, 2005), was a great help. Many thanks to Roger, who also responded kindly to my odd questions. Another useful site was www.porkbeinspired.com.

OTHER SOURCES

The quote on page 189 comes from Agnar Mykle's *Kjære lille Moff: Reisebrev fra Amerika* (Gyldendal, 2001). Otherwise, www.wikipedia.org, www.imdb.com, www.goodreads.com, and www.royalbaconsociety.com have been consulted frequently.

Photographs and illustrations not taken or drawn by the author are taken from www.thinkstock.com.

Visits to Grilstad in Brumunddal and FG Kjøttsenter in Groruddalen, along with the two trips to Norsvin in Hamar, have contributed to my understanding of the effort it takes to bring us proper bacon. A farm visit to Harald Gropen at Løken Østre was brief but enjoyable.